WHAT PEOPLE ARE SAYING ABOUT
CRAIG WALKER AND *REDISCOVERING YOU*...

Craig Walker is an unusual man. He is a local pastor of an incredible church who also has a vision for the world. Well over a million souls have found their way to the cross through his crusades that have evolved into digital events, and by speaking from the pulpit of his church, he is literally fulfilling the Great Commission to go into "all the world." In over fifty years of ministry, I have never met such a combination of a man. Now he has put pen to paper and has married segments of life and spiritual walk into a literal road map for the individual Christian to walk, develop, and prosper. In his new book *Rediscovering You*, Craig unlocks the door of opportunity that has been firmly closed, denying the church access to the keys of integration between our spiritual and natural lives. This book will light your mind and spirit to see things in a brand-new way. Hold on, your journey has just begun!

—*Philip Cameron*
Author, missionary, evangelist
TV host, *Daily Faith with Philip Cameron*

In *Rediscovering You*, Craig's years of wisdom as a pastor shines through as he talks about the Enneagram from a Christian perspective. You're sure to come away with an aha moment and a deeper perspective of what it means to be made in God's image.

—*Elisabeth Bennett*
Certified Enneagram Coach
Author, *60-Day Enneagram Devotional* series

CRAIG WALKER

REDISCOVERING YOU

SOLVING YOUR PERSONALITY PUZZLE TO ENHANCE YOUR LIFE

WHITAKER
HOUSE

Rediscovering You
Solving Your Personality Puzzle to Enhance Your Life

Upward Church
9859 N. Davis Highway
Pensacola, FL 32514
www.upwardchurch.org
www.youtube.com/c/UpwardChurch

ISBN: 978-1-64123-824-3
eBook ISBN: 978-1-64123-825-0

Printed in the United States of America
© 2022 by Craig Walker

Whitaker House
1030 Hunt Valley Circle
New Kensington, PA 15068
www.whitakerhouse.com

Library of Congress Cataloging-in-Publication Data (Pending)

1 2 3 4 5 6 7 8 9 10 11 ⨆⨆ 29 28 27 26 25 24 23 22

DEDICATION

This book is dedicated to our first grandchild, Nina Noel. We can't wait to meet you and discover who you are, and who you will become. While you are being knit together in your mother's womb, the favor of God is all upon you. We await your arrival with great joy!

CONTENTS

ACKNOWLEDGMENTS

Books are like tall sailing ships, for they demand the work of a highly skilled team to make them sail. I am deeply indebted to the marvelous team that has made this book a reality:

My editors Bekah Nelson, Candace Orlando, and Nancy O'Brien, you are the best!

Bradley Parker, your graphic design work is always superb.

I am so grateful for the entire team at Whitaker House for making this project all it should be.

My book agent Karen Hardin, I want to publicly thank you for the wise, straight-up, and valuable voice you bring to the table.

And finally, I owe so much to my sweetheart and bride Lezli Walker. You took my last name and my heart, and in return gave me a wonderful life. Thank you for all the glasses of unsweetened tea with your kind, gentle care that you brought to my writing table. I love you to the moon and back!

INTRODUCTION

Do you understand why you process things the way you do?

Did you know that your greatest fear often influences your decisions?

What is your Enneagram type? Are you a Reformer or a Peacemaker? What personality type is your spouse? Your children? Your close friends?

Discovering the answers to these questions will significantly enhance your life and your relationships.

As you read through the pages of this book, you will become equipped to paint a detailed and accurate self-portrait. We will use the Word of God, personality tests, the Enneagram, and love language tests to accomplish this. Separately, these tests cannot tell you everything, but together, these tools will help you to see yourself as you truly are.

Think of a one-thousand-piece puzzle. If you only look at one single piece, you can't see the big picture. Even fifty of them properly fitted together cannot give you that. However, when enough puzzle pieces are in place, you begin to realize what the complete picture will be like.

In the same way, when all of your test results are properly placed together, you will be equipped to honestly and accurately answer the question, "Who am I?" Possessing that answer changes everything, creating a ripple effect across all of your relationships.

Three decades of conducting counseling sessions taught me that self-awareness is the single greatest leap forward to better relationships and personal happiness. For this reason alone, I hope this is the most useful book you ever read—besides the Bible, of course.

 UNDERSTANDING YOUR WHY AND THE WHY OF OTHERS WILL CHANGE YOUR VIEW OF YOURSELF AND EVERY RELATIONSHIP YOU ARE IN.

Many riddles will be solved. Everything will begin to make sense once self-awareness is fully awakened. Understanding your *why* and the *why* of others will change your view of yourself and every relationship you are in. It is both fun and exhilarating to wake up to what feels like an entirely new world as you discover how you process, think, respond, and feel, and how everyone in your life reacts in the same or different ways.

In our time together, you will be asked to take the Enneagram test. If you are not familiar with Enneagram, it's a relational system of nine personality types. These include: One, the Reformer; Two, the Helper; Three, the Achiever; Four, the Individualist; Five, the Investigator; Six, the Loyalist; Seven, the Dreamer; Eight, the Challenger; and Nine, the Peacemaker.

Discovering your Enneagram type will prove to be both enlightening and life changing. I personally know many people who have experienced radical growth and relational improvement as a result of its use.

As we travel together, you will also be asked to take an assortment of other personality tests that will further help you to rediscover your true self. We will examine all of your test results through the lens of Scripture and then discuss biblical examples of each type.

This book is a tapestry of all these threads. This mosaic approach is necessary because none of these singular pieces can paint the entire picture. Independent of the others, each test result is a mere caricature of you. While each one will reveal some details, it is simply one piece of the puzzle. I am certain that the collective picture that you see when all of the pieces are assembled will help you understand yourself and others as never before.

If you examine the reverse side of a tapestry, it appears to be a confusing jumble of random threads of multiple colors. When you turn it over, however, you can see the intricate, beautiful image created by the weaver.

Similarly, the resources we use will appear to be random until they are tied together and turned over. The big picture created by these different elements will bring the real you into clear focus. This honest look in the mirror will allow us to work on our own flaws and imperfections to become the best version of ourselves possible. And when our own blemishes are brought to light, it's much easier to have more empathy for the flaws of others.

1

SELF-AWARENESS

If you could read just one book and improve all of your relationships, would you read it? Of course you would! This, I hope, is *that book*.

You see, *you* are the one common denominator in every relationship you have. Focusing on this ever-present factor is simply good math. Improve the one, and you improve them all. No one else can be your surrogate, or the connection is no longer your own. We are stuck with the person in the mirror, so let's get to know the nuances of our personality, love language, and Enneagram type, and thereby improve *all* of our relationships.

Our very best shot at healthy, vibrant, and growing relationships is found in understanding ourselves. I realized this truth one day after taking inventory of all the time-tested resources I had collected over the years to improve marital relationships. Each of them had one thing in common. In every case, each tool caused those who used them to understand themselves better. All of them! Proven books like Gary Chapman's *The 5 Love Languages*, *His Needs, Her Needs* by Willard F. Harley Jr., and Emerson Eggerichs' *Love & Respect* heightened the self-awareness of those who read them. Relationships benefited as a result.

> BECAUSE OUR PERCEPTION IS OUR REALITY, IT CAN BE DIFFICULT TO SEE OURSELVES AS WE REALLY ARE, THE WAY GOD SEES US.

Because *our perception is our reality*, it can be difficult to see ourselves as we really are, the way God sees us. Our reality is determined by our bias. The lenses through which we see ourselves must, therefore, be acknowledged and questioned. If not, we wrongly assume we see the whole picture. It is much like looking through the keyhole of a locked door into a beautiful room and somehow believing that we have seen all of its delights from such a limited view.

Understanding the lens through which we see, hear, and feel helps us to take a step back and ask, "Is this what the other person is saying, or is it how I am translating it?" We have to escape from our own perceptions because only then can we truly see others' viewpoints. Genuine human community is impossible when we hold onto our own prejudices, preconceived ideas, and feelings. We can open the door to really hearing what the other person is trying to communicate by breaking free from our own predetermined conclusions. This process starts by acknowledging that there are many different ways to see the same issue.

Many married people in highly committed relationships are often frustrated because they can't seem to get along. They genuinely love one another, but they struggle to keep peace in their homes. The opposites that once attracted each other have somehow become rubs that wear each other's nerves thin. Sadly, many just resign themselves to broken or less than ideal unions. A better self-awareness of how we think, process, and feel, *coupled* with discovering the same for others in our lives, can change everything.

Three decades ago, when I was a young pastor, I solved a riddle that was troubling me. In those early days of pastoring, every so often, different married couples would let me know that they would not be attending the weekend services because they were going on a marriage retreat. Upon hearing their news, I would often think quietly to myself, *Wow, I wish the couples I counseled last week would do something like that.* I wondered why those who needed it the most were far outdone by those who needed it the least.

Then one day, the riddle was solved. Over time, I saw a pattern develop. Consistently, those married couples in our congregation with the best relationships were the ones investing the most into their marriages. It suddenly occurred to me that these were the strongest relationships because they were contributing to them. Like a checking account, you can't make a withdrawal if you don't make deposits. These couples were giving entire weekends to invest in their marriages, and it was paying huge dividends. And the couples who typically required my counseling made little to no investment into their marriages—that is, until the account was overdrawn.

Similarly, the time you invest in this book will yield an exponential return *in all* of your relationships. The more you know yourself, the greater the return. True empathy blossoms from the soil of an unmasked heart. The clearer we see ourselves as we really are, the more we comprehend God's grace as truly amazing. With a heightened awareness of God's grace toward us, we become much more willing to extend grace and empathy to others and, as a result, deepen all our relationships.

Improved self-awareness even enables us to improve our relationship with Christ. Let me give you a practical example. I am a type Three on the Enneagram. This means that I am an

Achiever, driven by winning. This is most definitely the primary lens through which I view life. So, once I became aware of this, it helped me to pause and reexamine my perceived reality. The sacrifices I'm making, the cross I am bearing, is it really for Christ, or is it driven by my need to win? Our ministry has reached more than a million souls, but was it for my own need to achieve, or was it for Christ? Better self-awareness forced me to evaluate my motives. And though they can be shocking and painful to view, I find it far better to view them now than to see our works burn up on judgment day because our unconscious motives were not pure.

Many evangelicals have written off all attempts at self-awareness as simply navel-gazing or pseudoscience. Many never do the hard labor of stripping the soul down until it is naked and open, the way that God sees us. Abandoning the work of self-awareness forfeits the benefits that it alone can bring. Without this discipline, we remain lost in our own vain imagination of who we really are.

WITHOUT THE DISCIPLINE OF SELF-AWARENESS, WE REMAIN LOST IN OUR OWN VAIN IMAGINATION OF WHO WE REALLY ARE.

Far too little emphasis, especially in evangelical circles, has been given to dismantling the false self to find our new self in Christ. In *The Enneagram in Love and Work*, Helen Palmer notes, "A common prejudice still exists about self-observation. Many think of it as work for broken people rather than as a means for personal growth."[1]

Our habitual way of viewing and shaping life from our own egocentric viewpoint must be replaced. Our partial perspective cannot be allowed to be taken as a whole solution to anything in life. Somehow, we must escape from our self-centeredness to truly find God. We are made in *His* image, not the other way around.

---

1. Helen Palmer, *The Enneagram in Love and Work: Understanding Your Intimate and Business Relationships* (New York: HarperCollins Publishers, 1995), 4.

Unless we remove our distorted perceptions about ourselves and the people in our lives, we'll never be capable of seeing God as He truly is. In *The Enneagram: A Christian Perspective*, Richard Rohr and Andreas Ebert write:

> In our present-day egocentric society, we are especially inclined to remain stuck in our own thoughts or feelings. For this reason, God today is for many Westerners, unless they have dismissed God completely, nothing more than a projected image of themselves: a God that we desire, fear, or culturally need. The encounter with the Totally Other, with the Not-I, does not take place for most people.[2]

For me, writing a book about self-discovery is quite a startling, ironic turnaround. I was raised in the world of *deny yourself, take up your cross, and follow Jesus.* (See Matthew 16:24.) I was groomed in an environment that told us to *quit navel-gazing* and think only about others and Jesus.

But along this journey of more than thirty years of ministry experience, one truth concerning relationships became ever so evident: Until we first accurately know ourselves, we cannot completely fulfill the words of Jesus to *"Love the Lord your God with all your heart and with all your soul and with all your mind"* and *"Love your neighbor as yourself"* (Matthew 22:37, 39).

Until we regain what has been lost, it is impossible to love others by God's standards. Until we are first honest with ourselves, loving others as we love ourselves falls far short. A tainted view of who you really are will never fully allow you to complete the two greatest commandments that Christ gave us.

In no way am I minimizing our need to take up our cross to follow Jesus. Truly, there is a cross for all of us to bear. But until we understand *who* we are, we don't really know *who* it is we are

---

2. Richard Rohr and Andreas Ebert, *The Enneagram: A Christian Perspective* (New York: Crossroad Publishing Company, 2019), 21.

nailing to the cross or *what* it is that we are denying ourselves. Our unconscious motives become clearer as we can discern who we are and how we are "*fearfully and wonderfully made*" (Psalm 139:14).

THE JOURNEY OF SELF-DISCOVERY CAN BE PAINFUL, SHOWING US FLAWS THAT WE WOULD RATHER NOT INSPECT.

I forewarn you that while many people enjoy the journey of self-discovery, it can also be painful. In my own observation, those who benefit the most from understanding their true selves are often the ones who are the most opposed to that discovery. The revelation can show them flaws that they would rather not inspect. If that is where you find yourself, I encourage you to press on. The rewards will far outweigh the discomfort.

In my last book, *Born for the Extraordinary*,[3] I highlighted the breadcrumbs that our Creator left on life's path to lead us toward His purposes. Much was said about how to know God's specific will for your life, His prearranged path to your extraordinary destiny. I believe this book will make that path even clearer.

The next chapters should be read and internalized before you take any tests. Please don't skip ahead, or your results may be incorrect. If you have already taken some of these tests in the past, I ask that you read the following chapters and then retake them.

It's now time for a grand adventure into *Rediscovering You*. Like Dorothy in *The Wizard of Oz*, we must begin by traveling down the yellow brick road of our fantasies—the lies we tell ourselves. If you make the journey, you will discover the real you and find your way home.

---

3. Craig Walker, *Born for the Extraordinary: When Your Life Aligns with His Purpose* (Shippensburg, PA: Harrison House, 2021).

2

A CASE OF MISTAKEN IDENTITY

Before we can dive into your Enneagram type and other personality traits, it is absolutely critical that we first deal with the subject of mistaken identity.

We spend our lives telling ourselves stories that fit into what we want to believe about ourselves. All of us do it. Although sometimes intentional and in other instances completely without our conscious knowledge, we spin tales that fit the constructs of who we would *like* to be rather than who we *truly are*. We start with a make-believe narrative and then build a false identity that we find attractive. This becomes our life-lie, the mask we wear that skews our view of our true self and limits our view of others.

Sadly, we believe that the more precisely we adhere to this false identity, the more valuable we become. Unable to keep up the illusion for the long term, we work even harder to reinforce it. The lies then multiply and build up layers. It is for this reason that we often see ourselves differently than the evidence supports. Please don't think, "This isn't me; I can skip this chapter." It *is* you—*and* me and everyone else in this world. You could jump ahead and utilize the tools given, but if you are looking with skewed vision, you will only increase your own self-deception.

When we lie to ourselves about who we really are, we have a case of mistaken identity. We unintentionally become self-deceived. As in *Alice in Wonderland*, the looking glass becomes a gateway into a fantasy world rather than an accurate reflection of our identity. The deeper down the rabbit hole we go, the more difficult it becomes to find our way back to reality. Many have followed this path and have lost their true self along the way.

This *true self* is the person we were created to be, in the very image of God, before the fall. When God created Adam and Eve, they were complete, whole, and without sin. Their innocence was so complete that they were physically naked and felt no need to hide or cover up. Their identity was free from all false constructs. In this state, God declared all of His creation good.

> BEFORE SIN ENTERED OUR WORLD, ADAM AND EVE WERE FREE FROM THE MASKS WE WEAR AND THE LIES WE TELL OURSELVES. THEY WERE LIBERATED FROM ALL SELF-DECEPTION.

Before sin entered our world, Adam and Eve were free from the masks we wear and the lies we tell ourselves. They functioned as their true selves, liberated from all self-deception. They perfectly reflected the image of God in their own unique way. This is what God has set out to restore in all of us.

God's redemptive plan is to restore *all* that was lost in the garden of Eden. He desires to live and walk among us now and throughout all eternity. To do this, He must guide us back to our true selves, free from all of the deceptions and masks we hide behind. God sent the Holy Spirit to lead and guide us into all truth. (See John 16:13.) His plan made way for all of paradise to be restored, including the removal of the masks that hide His image from being seen in us. Grace removes all the shame of our past, so we no longer feel the need to hide from Him, as Adam and Eve did after their disobedience. With the redemptive work of Christ and the Holy Spirit's help, we can find our way back to our original created selves.

What complicates our journey back is the fact that the one deceiving us, more often than not, is the person in the mirror. It is not some slick salesman with whom our defenses are held on high alert. No, if we are being honest, it is the person we care the most about, the one reflected in the looking glass. For this reason, we may require outside resources and the Holy Spirit to rescue us from our own carefully crafted inward deceptions. This chapter is intended to help us identify, acknowledge, and abandon the lies we tell ourselves about who we really are. On our journey together, we will utilize many powerful tools and rely upon the Holy Spirit to guide us. When put to use, these are some of the most effective devices I have ever encountered.

I encourage you to stay the course. It can be excruciating to see what lies under the mask. You can feel very exposed and vulnerable when the makeup is removed. Yet, our true beauty cannot be restored until we are first honest with ourselves. This can prove to be a painful chapter for some, but paradise restored is waiting on the other side if you will forge up the misty mountain.

We don't need another layer of paint to spruce up our false facades. We need to be redeemed and then stripped down to our original state. That is where our true grandeur shines in all of its brilliance. This is where we reflect the very image of God in our own unique way. He made you beautiful as you truly are.

Before we begin this process, we must first attempt to disassemble all of the false constructs we have made that shroud our true identity. We must start here, or all of our test results will be skewed. Until we disassemble the false narratives, we are seeing a false image—the back of the tapestry, the puzzle pieces in a pile. We can assemble a picture of our true selves by applying Scripture, the Enneagram test, the five love languages test, and a few more resources. Together, they will give us an accurate reflection of who we are meant to be, liberating us from the lies that hold us captive.

So...who are you really? What is your response when asked to define yourself? None of the things we are about to discuss are bad in and of themselves. The deception only takes place when we contextualize our whole life through any one of them independent of the rest.

> HERE ARE THREE LIES WE OFTEN TELL OURSELVES ABOUT WHO WE ARE: I AM WHAT I DO; I AM WHAT OTHERS SAY ABOUT ME; AND I AM WHAT I HAVE.

A Dutch priest named Henri Nouwen revealed three lies we often tell ourselves about who we are:

1. I am what I do.
2. I am what others say about me.
3. I am what I have.

Finding our identity solely through any one of these three fabrications limits our ability to love ourselves correctly and fully love others. We make room for God's calling and purpose in our lives when we dismantle these lies that are warping our identity.

The first lie, "I am what I do," is often encapsulated by a narrower belief such as, "I am a student working on finishing up my degree," or "I am an employee who works hard in my field and excels at what I do," or "I am a mother who manages my household and ensures that my family's needs are met." But these are all things that you *do*; they are not who you *are*.

As we get older and can *do* far less, those who find their identity in "I am what I do" face a grim future. The moment you are unable to keep up the pace, who are you then? Left unchecked, this lie one day will be even more devastating and turn into "I am what I *did*."

When accomplishments become things of the past, those trapped in this lie find life incredibly empty. Many come to the end of their lives sad and lost because they no longer feel useful. The natural deficiency already felt due to their waning usefulness is further aggravated by an identity crisis. They are left to ask, "Who am I now that I am no longer doing?"

Relationships viewed through this false identity recede in value as well. They become so hollow that you ask, "What have I done for you lately?" or even "What have *you* done for *me*?"

The second lie, "I am what others say about me," can manifest as such concepts as "I'm seen as a loving person," or "People appreciate me for my hard work and achievements," or "I am admired for my personality and my unique contributions to the lives of others." This is by far the most external of the three lies because we are fully at the mercy of our observers when we find ourselves in this deception. This results in precariously fragile self-worth, held up only by the opinions of others. *"Jesus did not commit Himself"* to men (John 2:24 NKJV) because He knew that just days after the people shouted, "Hosanna," they would scream, "Crucify Him!" (See John 12:12–13; 19:15.)

The third lie, "I am what I have," can have us believing a multitude of things, such as:

+ "I have my health."
+ "I have great relationships with my loved ones."
+ "I have the knowledge I need to traverse this life safely."
+ "I have enough saved up to retire."

Like the previous lies, these things can be a great *part* of a rich, fulfilling life, but like the others, they only last as long as you have them. When your health fades…when family ties are fractured…when you don't have the answers…when your investments go belly-up… What do you have then?

I'm guessing that you are feeling a little sting from one of these three false identities. It is quite easy to fall into their traps. The heart of the matter is that all of these lies are finite; they will not endure, and we are still left with the nagging question, "Who am I?"

As it turns out, we have the ultimate resource for gaining an eternal perspective and finding our true identity. Our Creator has given us our divine blueprints:

> *In the same way we also, when we were children, were enslaved to the elementary principles of the world. But when the fullness of time had come, God sent forth his Son, born of woman, born under the law, to redeem those who were under the law, so that we might receive adoption as sons.*
>
> (Galatians 4:3–5 ESV)

We can break this Scripture down to this simple phrase: you were created to be a son or daughter of God. Just as children resemble their natural parents, we were made in the image of God and should resemble Him. This is where we can find our true identity.

God desires to adopt us back into His family so we can find our true selves. Paul's reference to adoption can be found elsewhere in the Bible:

> *For those who are led by the Spirit of God are the children of God. The Spirit you received does not make you slaves, so that you live in fear again; rather, the Spirit you received brought about your adoption to sonship. And by him we cry, "Abba, Father."*
>
> (Romans 8:14–15)

During Paul's day, a Roman man without a child would adopt an heir. A few things happened as soon as the adoption was complete. First, the man would cancel any debt that this son had. The son received a new name and became heir of all that his new father possessed. Then, his new father became liable for all his actions, and the new son had an obligation to please and honor his father.

WHEN WE LIVE WITH AN ETERNAL PERSPECTIVE, OUR FINITE TIME HERE ON EARTH BECOMES ALL THE MORE MEANINGFUL.

When we live with an *eternal* perspective, our finite time here on earth becomes all the more meaningful. Our identity and purpose migrate from the limited span of a lifetime to the limitless boundaries of eternity when we understand that we are children of God.

Through this lens, we can be honest with ourselves and accurately take the tests we are about to begin. We no longer need to hide behind false constructs. We can dare to be open and honest with ourselves. It is only when our identity is found in being a child of God—knowing that sin has twisted us, but also knowing that Jesus came to redeem us entirely—that we can lay aside our masks and become brutally honest with ourselves, others, and our Creator.

A WORSHIP LEADER'S TESTIMONY

The following is the personal testimony of a worship leader from Florida who finally broke free from the lies we tell ourselves. By dismantling his own false identity, he grew exponentially in Christ.

—

The year I turned twenty-eight, I decided I wanted to finish the things that I started. I began reading about the Enneagram. It is a personality test based on how we express ourselves and process the world emotionally. I enjoy the Enneagram because it gives each of the nine types a lot to think about. Much of it can be really tough to hear, but it is incredibly freeing to feel so understood.

The Enneagram gives me a lot to work on so I can continue my path of personal growth. It also has provided me with incredible empathy for all the other eight Enneagram types.

I am a type Five on the Enneagram, which is commonly called the Investigator. Type Five brains are constantly going a hundred miles an hour. They are constantly thinking—thinking, thinking, and more thinking...

As I pondered this, it hit me, "What have I been thinking about for the last ten years?" The answer felt like a gut punch. The truthful answer was, "Nothing that really mattered." I wasted my time outside of church on TV, video games, and hobbies. I had zero moderation, zero eternal bearings. I was utterly selfish and barely read my Bible.

I was trapped in the three lies cited by Henri Nouwen, and they let me feel like I had things figured out. I am what I do; I work for a church. I am what I have—a comfortable life and independence. I am what others say I am; I serve God by leading worship, and I create beautiful wedding videos that express my creativity.

It took me ten years to realize I was bearing the name of Christ yet still living my own life. I was bearing the name Christian, which means "little Christ," but bearing His name in vain.

The late evangelist Nabeel Qureshi said, "Taking the Lord's name in vain doesn't mean stubbing your toe and then saying, 'Oh God.' It means bearing the name of Christ and not living by his teachings."

The Enneagram helped me to open my eyes to the truth. I can no longer bear to live on my terms anymore. I can feel a fire burning inside of me now. The fire was always there, but it was nothing but embers. The phrase "No turning back" has so much more meaning now. Now every Bible verse I read, every apologetics video I watch, and every book I finish feels like I'm throwing another log on the fire.

All of us who are Christians have that fire in us. Many have tended to their fire well, but many have not. Jesus said, "*I know your works: you are neither cold nor hot. Would that you were either cold or hot! So because you are lukewarm, and neither hot nor cold, I will spit you out of my mouth*" (Revelation 3:15–16 ESV). It can be easy to forget all that God has done, to slip back into our own comfortable routine. We all have to tend to our fires continually! It is an ongoing work.

Be on the lookout for these three lies in your own life. They are aspects of you, but they are not who you are! Tend to your fires, and chase after God.

—

You can hear the passion in this young man's words. The Holy Spirit used this one tool to make a radical difference in his life. It helped him to see through his false illusions. Once the fog lifted, he could begin the journey back toward his true self.

Understanding how lost we can become in Oz, a world of fantasy, further accentuates the importance of accurate self-awareness. Ask the Holy Spirit to enable you to be truthful with yourself as we go into the next section. Ask Him to guide you in answering your test questions honestly. It will pay big dividends for those who are brave enough to try. Like Dorothy, let's stop the madness and find our way back. Let this worship leader's example inspire you because we all know, "There is no place like home."

3

A BRIEF DESCRIPTION OF
THE ENNEAGRAM

My prayer is that the last chapter gave you a deep desire to be brutally honest with yourself as we proceed with one of the most important parts of our journey together. You will be asked to take a series of free exams on the Internet, starting with an Enneagram test.

The Enneagram is an ancient typology that identifies nine different general personality profiles. I have devoted an entire chapter to each Enneagram type. Each profile is a general outline of those who fit within it. Not every facet found within each description will apply to every individual within that group. They are only rough sketches that allow us to find ourselves within our specific type. Some profiles will be easy to eliminate from consideration when determining your own type because their descriptions clearly do not represent you.

The nine types of the Enneagram are often expressed as follows: One, the Reformer; Two, the Helper; Three, the Achiever; Four, the Individualist; Five, the Investigator; Six, the Loyalist; Seven, the Dreamer; Eight, the Challenger; and Nine, the Peacemaker. Some Enneagram teachers use other names for these types, such as Perfectionist for One, or Enthusiast for Seven.

It is important to note that experts agree that, unlike temperament, our dominant Enneagram type does not change but stays with us throughout our lives. Since it doesn't change, we should strive to maintain an awareness of the particular lenses through which we see life.

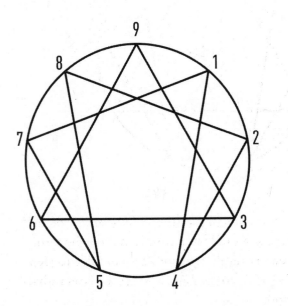

1. REFORMER
2. HELPER
3. ACHIEVER
4. INDIVIDUALIST
5. INVESTIGATOR
6. LOYALIST
7. DREAMER
8. CHALLENGER
9. PEACEMAKER

We are all dominant in just one of these nine types. The word "Enneagram" derives its meaning from two Greek words: *ennea* meaning "nine," and *gramma*, meaning a sign that is "drawn" or "written." (The word "diagram" is also derived from the latter.)

Represented by a circle, the Enneagram has an equilateral triangle in its center and nine points forty degrees distant from one another on the circle's circumference. These points are numbered clockwise from one to nine on the circle, with nine at the twelve o'clock position. An equilateral triangle connects points three, six, and nine. Two, four, one, seven, five, and eight make an irregular hexagram symbol. The points represent how each number corresponds with its connected type.

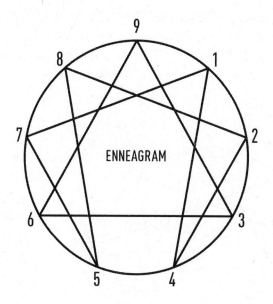

Many have found the insights of the Enneagram to be life changing. You will read some of their testimonies throughout this book. They all adamantly testify that they are now able to view themselves and others with eye-opening clarity, far beyond what they experienced before.

THE ENNEAGRAM ILLUMINATES OUR CHARACTER AND HIDDEN MOTIVES, ENABLING US TO RELATE TO OTHERS IN AN ENTIRELY NEW WAY.

The Enneagram is extraordinarily precise. It illuminates our character and hidden motives. This illumination enables us to relate to others in an entirely new way. Empathy and compassion replace our judgments of what we previously perceived as others' faults. It allows us to walk in their shoes and see the world through the lenses that they wear. The biases we hold against others whose personalities are not like ours reveal that we are prejudging them based on opinions that often have nothing to do with reality.

DISCOVERING OUR TYPE

The first step in completing your tapestry or puzzle is discovering your own Enneagram type. The "prominent need" of the nine Enneagram types is often more helpful in uncovering your own type than even the names commonly associated with each of them. The following chart shows the major needs of each type.

TYPE	BASIC NEED
One	The Need to Be Perfect
Two	The Need to Be Needed
Three	The Need to Succeed
Four	The Need to Be Special (or Unique)
Five	The Need to Perceive (or Understand)
Six	The Need to Be Sure/Certain (or Secure)
Seven	The Need to Avoid Pain
Eight	The Need to Be Against
Nine	The Need to Avoid

What is *your* greatest need?

Another helpful way to determine your Enneagram type is to look at the idealization of the nine types. We do this by finishing the statement, "I am good when I am..." The answer you most identify with is beneficial in pinpointing your type. Here are the nine answers associated with each type:

1. Ones: I am good when I am honest, hard-working, and orderly.

2. Twos: I am good when I am loving, selfless, and helpful.

3. Threes: I am good when I am successful, competent, and effective.

4. Fours: I am good when I am original, sensitive, and cultured.

5. Fives: I am good when I am wise, smart, and receptive.

6. Sixes: I am good when I am faithful, obedient, and loyal.

7. Sevens: I am good when I am optimistic, happy, and nice.

8. Eights: I am good when I am strong and dominant.

9. Nines: I am good when I am calm, in harmony, and balanced.

What is most important to you? How would you complete this sentence, "I am good when I..."?

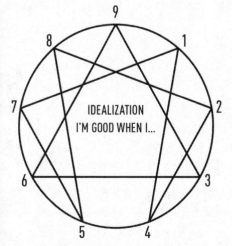

1. AM HONEST, HARDWORKING, AND ORDERLY
2. AM LOVING, SELFLESS, AND HELPFUL
3. AM SUCESSFUL, COMPETENT, AND EFFECTIVE
4. AM ORIGINAL, SENSITIVE, AND CULTURED
5. AM WISE, SMART, AND RECEPTIVE
6. AM FAITHFUL, OBEDIENT, AND LOYAL
7. AM OPTIMISTIC, HAPPY, AND NICE
8. AM JUST, STRONG, AND DOMINANT
9. AM CALM, IN HARMONY, AND BALANCED

In addition to your prominent need and idealization, the prominent fear of each type will also aid us in recognizing our particular number on the Enneagram. The greatest fear of all types can be found on the following chart.

TYPE	BASIC FEAR
One	Of being bad, imbalance, defective, corrupt
Two	Of being unloved
Three	Of being worthless, without inherent value
Four	Of having no identity or significance
Five	Of being helpless, incompetent, and incapable
Six	Of being without support and guidance
Seven	Of being trapped in pain and deprivation
Eight	Of being harmed, controlled, and violated
Nine	Of being lost, separated, and fragmented

THE WINGS FROM ADJACENT TYPES

The neighboring numbers directly flanking ours on the Enneagram circle are known as our "wings." These adjacent types help to balance us, highlighting the best version of our type. Leaning into and developing our wings can transform us into healthier individuals. For example, a One who leans into their Nine wing can lay down their striving for perfection and be at rest in the peaceful realization that perfection is a process, a journey that we are all on. Growth becomes acceptable, in spite of the imperfections. The One who leans into their Nine wing will find peace.

When thinking about your type's wings, it's helpful to envision someone walking on a tightrope with a balancing pole. At times, to find his balance, the funambulist will raise one arm high while dropping the other. He will lean to one side or the other to find his equilibrium. When we are mentally, emotionally, and spiritually healthy, we can use our Enneagram wings to take a more balanced approach to life.

> WHEN WE ARE MENTALLY, EMOTIONALLY, AND SPIRITUALLY HEALTHY, WE CAN USE OUR ENNEAGRAM WINGS TO TAKE A MORE BALANCED APPROACH TO LIFE.

A heightened awareness of our wings, combined with our type, can expedite real personal growth. During the different stages of life, it is not uncommon to notice that your dominance can fluctuate between one wing or the other. Experts believe that it is common for one of the wings to develop in the first half of life. A holistic goal and endeavor is to develop both wings, which usually doesn't occur until the second half of life.

While determining your type, if you are unsure of your dominant number because you vacillate between two numbers separated by a third, you are probably the middle number. For example, those unsure if they are a Nine or a Two are likely a One. If you have two neighboring numbers that appear to be your type, you have likely identified your actual type and one of your wings. So now you can see that the wings are actually helpful in determining your actual Enneagram number.

MOVING FORWARD

Following the advice of those who possess far more knowledge about the Enneagram than I do, I ask that you read the descriptions of each number and try to identify your type before taking the test. Many have discovered their type by simply reading the descriptions, responding with, "Oh my goodness, that is so me!"

The nine points represent nine mirrors that expose the illusions that define our sense of self. By looking at each of these mirrors, we expose the nine masks commonly worn. They help us to discover our true motives, providing an escape route from the self-deception of our false self. When we honestly comprehend them, we see our utter and total need for a Savior. They shake us out of our dream world and into the reality of our own spiritual poverty. Finding our way to our true home with God begins by identifying the mask, acknowledging the lies we tell ourselves and others, and then repenting to the One who paid for the wages of those sins.

Like waking up from deep sleep, or coming out from under the effects of anesthesia after surgery, the Enneagram awakens us from our unconsciousness. It is smelling salts for the soul, helping us to shake off the disguises we all wear. In *The Enneagram: A Christian Perspective*, Richard Rohr and Andreas Ebert write, "Ernest Becker called it 'our vital lie.' Merton called it the false self. The Enneagram gets right to the point and calls it our sin."[4]

HUMILIATION AND PAIN

There will be great pleasure in becoming more self-aware with the Enneagram, but expect some humiliation and pain as well. In fact, the more humiliating you find it, the more accurately you are perceiving it. Those who don't find it so are not really comprehending it. The Enneagram is meant to strip us of the disguises we hide behind and expose them so that we can rid ourselves of the lies we have let define us. Those who are still enamored with the disguise have missed the point.

If you are an Eight, the Challenger, probably nothing I say can convince you to take a look at the Enneagram, but I *challenge* you to try it anyway. The vulnerability required to take an honest look inside ourselves stops many Eights from trying; their basic need to oppose and their basic fear of being harmed or controlled makes them avoid such openness. But I hope you will accept the challenge and discover how helpful the Enneagram can be.

4. Rohr and Ebert, *The Enneagram: A Christian Perspective*, xix.

The Enneagram even exposes where we have done the right things with wrong motives. This is a large part of the humiliation that it brings. It is both freeing and humbling all at the same time. It should be taken as far more than an interesting exercise in self-discovery. The key is to recognize wrong motives, repent of them, and let them go.

OBJECTIONS TO THE ENNEAGRAM

Let me state what should be obvious to those who follow Christ: the Enneagram cannot put you in right standing with God. No amount of looking inside of yourself can redeem you. The Bible says, *"For all have sinned and fall short of the glory of God"* (Romans 3:23). We all stand guilty before God, and there is only one remedy. *"The wages of sin is death, but the gift of God is eternal life in Christ Jesus our Lord"* (Romans 6:23). The sacrificial Lamb, Jesus, the Son of God, died in our place and paid our debt because *"without shedding of blood there is no remission"* (Hebrews 9:22 NKJV).

> THE ENNEAGRAM EXPOSES OUR PERSONALITIES THAT HAVE BEEN DISTORTED BY SIN SO THAT WE CAN RUN TO CHRIST AND FIND GRACE, FORGIVENESS, AND TRANSFORMATION.

No attempt is being made to make the Enneagram anything more than it is—a tool that enables us to see behind the polished masks of false identity that we all wear. It exposes our personalities that have been distorted by sin so that we can run to Christ and find grace, forgiveness, and transformation through our Savior. The Enneagram exposes how we interact with our world; it helps us understand others' vantage points and makes us even more thankful that God loves us in our broken condition.

It is not some mystical approach to the inner soul, but rather a mirror. To make the Enneagram more than this is a mistake and a perversion of the help it offers. Much of the opposition and criticism toward the Enneagram exists because people have attempted to make it out to be something else.

HISTORY AND TRUTH

One objection to the Enneagram is its much-discussed past. Its origins have caused many to dismiss it entirely. The Enneagram's origin is hotly debated, but it is important to note that all *truth* ultimately comes from God. Even when a scientific atheist makes a discovery, it is still God's truth. We do not reject the facts solely because the scientist rejects or defies God. The truth still belongs to God, and it cannot be negated by the spiritual state of the one who found it.

Certainly, all truth can quickly be perverted into a lie. This is an old trick that dates all the way back to the garden of Eden and the original temptation, when the serpent asked Eve, *"Did God really say..."* (Genesis 3:1). Humans have an amazing ability to turn any truth into a lie, and Satan, the father of all lies, is always ready to distort the next nugget of God's revelation that we receive.

The same holds true for the Enneagram. Some have taken its value and stretched it beyond its usefulness. Like all truth, it has been perverted, misinterpreted, and misused. But rejecting it on those grounds is like breaking a mirror because you don't like what you see.

There are those who insist that the Enneagram should be rejected entirely because some use it as its own religion or as a substitute for the gospel. This is the same faulty logic that Paul had to address in his letter to the Corinthians. Many of the young Christians at that time believed that they could not eat food that had been offered to idols. Paul told them, *"Food does not commend us to God; for neither if we eat are we the better, nor if we do not eat are we the worse"* (1 Corinthians 8:8 NKJV). In essence, he is saying,

"Don't throw good things away simply because misguided people have used it in their false religion." That is what those who reject the Enneagram are doing. Because it has been misused, they reject its usefulness entirely.

Let me be clear: the Enneagram is merely a tool we can use to help us. It is not a pathway to God or a means of redemption or transformation. Only the blood of Jesus can redeem us. Only Christ can transform us.

> WE MUST FILTER THE DISCOVERIES WE MAKE WITH THE ENNEAGRAM THROUGH THE ABSOLUTE TRUTH OF GOD'S WORD.

As with all claims, we must filter the discoveries we make with the Enneagram through the absolute truth of God's Word. Just as a miner pans for gold, we take the real treasure and discard the rest. Eat the wheat and burn the chaff. The Enneagram is a marvelous tool to help us understand ourselves and others better, but the Holy Spirit is the Guide who leads us into all truth. It is true that we don't need the Enneagram to dismantle our false self, but many have found this to be an invaluable resource in their journey toward their own liberation.

CAPITAL SIN

Another objection to the Enneagram is the fact that it speaks of our *capital sin* or compulsion. While many have debated what this means, the idea originates from the belief that our limited perspective is the whole picture. This belief is our self-delusion, our own particular brand of self-centeredness.

Our compulsion is like wearing rose-colored glasses, seeing all of the world with a rosy tint but remaining somehow oblivious that this is the case. Our inner motives are left hidden until these deceptive lenses are removed. The underlying drives of our personalities keep us from understanding ourselves, thus hindering us from truly reflecting the image of our Creator. We cannot accurately bear the image of Christ until we dismantle these hidden sins.

Reconciliation with God, our neighbors, and ourselves is possible. The Holy Spirit can use the Enneagram to expose our own particular compulsion and brand of self-centeredness. Acknowledgment and repentance of our sinfulness grant us access to Christ's grace that is freely given.

By simply naming something correctly, we are given some measure of power over it. Identifying the mask we are wearing unlocks the cell of false identity. Left undetected, these compulsions continue to influence how we relate to others; once exposed, we have the freedom to decide whether we wish to continue granting power to our own self-delusions. Personal growth and freedom become more readily achievable with the awareness of our own particular brand of self-centeredness. These compulsions have been so carefully hidden that we must be intentional in our efforts to expose them.

Once our self-centeredness is exposed, we can ask God for forgiveness and put Him back in His rightful place at the center of our lives. This is the place where paradise is restored in our hearts, where we find our way home to our true self. This is the place where Adam and Eve were before their fall. The best part is, God's redemptive power is not limited only to heaven, but it is complete now! Jesus said, *"It is finished"* (John 19:30), and it was! With true repentance, sin loses all its power *now*.

The whole process of repentance cannot even begin until there is an acknowledgment of our sin. The Enneagram can be very useful in this acknowledgment. The Bible asks the question, *"The heart is deceitful above all things, and desperately wicked; who can know it?"* (Jeremiah 17:9 NKJV). The correct answer is *no one*—not without the Holy Spirit. As we see in John 16:8, the Holy Spirit was sent to convince and convict us of our sins. He uses tools such as the Enneagram to expose the false self that is grounded in our self-centeredness. The Holy Spirit is restoring paradise now in the hearts of His people, returning His children to the image of God as we reflect Christ.

Surely, fallen men will fall again. We will drift back to self-centeredness. This is why the humble state of repentance must be a daily, continual walk for us. We must be *"crucified with Christ"* (Galatians 2:20), nailing our old self to the cross and saying with the apostle Paul, *"I die daily"* (1 Corinthians 15:31 NKJV). We must strive to say with Paul, *"The life I now live in the body, I live by faith in the Son of God, who loved me and gave himself for me"* (Galatians 2:20).

The good news is that when we fall, *"we have an advocate with the Father—Jesus Christ, the Righteous One"* (1 John 2:1). He is our Mediator, the administrator of a new covenant, and a high priest, *"For by one offering He has perfected forever those who are being sanctified"* (Hebrews 10:14 NKJV). His grace is more than enough to cover all of our sins as we continually repent of our self-centeredness.

When our *false self* is exposed, the three lies we tell ourselves about our identity lose their power. We find we don't need those lies anymore because identifying as a child of God is enough. With our gaze turned away from that false self, we begin to focus on the essential truth of who we are in God and who we were created to be, leaving behind the crutches that have propped us up for far too long.

> WITH OUR GAZE TURNED AWAY FROM OUR FALSE SELF,
> WE BEGIN TO FOCUS ON THE ESSENTIAL TRUTH OF WHO WE ARE IN
> GOD AND WHO WE WERE CREATED TO BE.

This journey of discovery helps us understand where others are coming from, and how they relate to their world through their own skewed vision. This awareness makes us more capable of loving other people, loving ourselves, and loving God. The wisdom of the Enneagram is undeniably compelling.

When everything is weighed and judged by our own limited perspective, the beauty of God's complete creation is misrepresented. Only from the humble stance of "I only see in part" can we begin to view ourselves and others as God sees us. To perceive from all nine different vantage points is to look through the eyes of God. I believe Adam and Eve had this capability before the fall, before the image-bearers lost their innocence.

Stepping back to explore the world from all nine Enneagram vantage points takes wisdom and discernment. Those who are trapped in themselves cannot see from this broader perspective. Indeed, the further the Enneagram type is from your own, the more alien their viewpoint will seem. As we become more centered in Christ, we move away from our own self illusions while simultaneously growing in our capacity to accurately perceive other people's outlooks.

Occasionally, you meet people who are *"quick to listen, slow to speak"* (James 1:19). They have an inner peace that causes them to be active and yet neutral when engaged in a conversation. Not given to rash judgment, they recognize that *"to answer before listening—that is folly and shame"* (Proverbs 18:13). They inwardly know that there are multiple ways to perceive a matter. It seems they can read you and know right where you are coming from.

I believe this is one of the greatest benefits of the Enneagram—to see through the eyes of others, enriching your relationships.

Compassion and grace flow from understanding. For example, when we recognize that type Ones are harder on themselves than anyone else and that they are trying hard to put into order what is wrong in the world, we find that compassion replaces what once was disdain for their critical eyes. We are more receptive to their critiques once we become aware that their own inner critic never relents. They need our empathy, not our angst. They deserve our appreciation for their great gift of perception that can readily identify what is out of place in our world. God bless them!

We all have work to do. Let's ask the Holy Spirit to help us as we begin reading the descriptions of each Enneagram type. Once completed, you will be directed to take one of the many Enneagram tests available. By identifying our dominant vantage point—the lens through which we view our world—we can temporarily remove our self-delusions and see the world differently, perhaps as you have never viewed it before.

> **THERE ARE NO WRONG OR RIGHT ENNEAGRAM TYPES. TO BELIEVE SO IS TO BELIEVE THAT GOD MAKES MISTAKES.**

Before you read the following Enneagram types, you must settle in your heart and mind that *there are no wrong or right types.* To believe so is to believe that God makes mistakes. No one type is better than another. We are each made in the very image of God, and that remains true even if sin has perverted that image.

The Enneagram is a tool to help us find our way back to a proper reflection of our Creator. By surrendering it all to Jesus and then cooperating with the Holy Spirit, we are transformed into the image of Christ. We call that being God-centered, not self-centered.

When redeemed, each type reflects a virtue of God in their own unique way as only they can. Each type offers an invaluable contribution to our world and those in it. For example, my dear wife Lezli is a type One, while I am a type Three. Lezli, true to her type, can quickly recognize when something is out of place or missing. Her keen perception has been invaluable to me as a pastor over the years. There are many things I would have missed and many people who needed a personal touch that would have been unintentionally unseen had God not given me the helpmate I needed. My type One helpmate keeps everything in its place and runs a tight ship. The Three in me can stay busy achieving because I never need to worry about our lives disintegrating into chaos. Lezli brings order and balance into my whirlwind. We could have never separately accomplished what we have achieved together. We are a team that is far better together than apart.

We each have a role to play; God has a specific duty and place for all of us. The world is less without you, and you are far more when you are in your rightful place within it. Whatever type you may be, God made you in His image, with your own unique gifts and talents. You were born in this generation by God's design. The Bible says:

> *From one man he made all the nations, that they should inhabit the whole earth; and he marked out their appointed times in history and the boundaries of their lands.*
>
> (Acts 17:26)

God placed each of us in the specific generation with our own distinctive traits so that we can make the greatest impact for His glory. We are not random DNA, nor are we randomly placed in time. And we are most certainly not mistakes or rejects. As I wrote in my last book *Born for the Extraordinary*:

> Our Creator has stamped His watermark upon each of our lives. A watermark is "a translucent design impressed on paper during manufacturing, invisible until the paper is held to the light." The potential to display our heavenly Father's watermark resides in each of us. The light of Jesus illuminates it.
>
> The purpose of a watermark is to identify an original from a counterfeit. I bought a purse for my wife in Italy in an open square. The panhandler assured me that it was

made of the "highest quality genuine Italian leather." We wish it had a watermark on it of some kind to tell the real from the counterfeit. We still have nagging doubts that this purse is all it was promised to be. Have you ever felt that way about the life you are currently living?

Every human comes with God's watermark, only visible when held in the light of Jesus. We are made in the image of God—each an original. If we choose a life without His mark on display, we live a counterfeit version of what God has planned for us—a life of far less value. In this condition, we are not living our God-given destiny. Only a small portion of His image is visible when walking outside of His design. Choosing our own path causes His image to be blurred. We remain merely semi-transparent. It is difficult to see the Creator's design without His watermark illuminated. It is impossible to live the great adventure God pre-planned for us when it is missing.

Jesus Christ is the Father's watermark, "the exact representation of His being" (Hebrews 1:3 NIV). When our steps are squarely in the Father's will, Jesus shines through us. Your very best life is realized when His watermark is the most evident in you.

Just as photographers twist and adjust the lens of a camera to bring their subjects into focus, we too can view our God-given destiny with great precision and clarity. When properly dialed in, we can live our highest potential for maximum impact in the generation in which we live.[5]

Don't lament or try to change your Enneagram type—that won't work anyway—but embrace it and determine to be the healthiest version of you that you can be. Lean into your wings.

---

5. Walker, *Born for the Extraordinary*, 15–16.

Bring your unique gifts and talents to the table, and don't bury them.

BEING HEALTHY IN OUR TYPE

To reiterate, the Enneagram symbol consists of a circle with connecting lines. Going clockwise from the twelve o'clock position, an equilateral triangle connects nine, three, and six. Two, four, one, seven, five, and eight connect to make an irregular hexagram. The Enneagram symbol has roots in antiquity and can be traced as far back as Greek philosopher and mathematician Pythagoras.

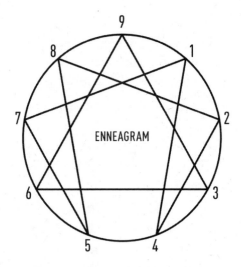

The lines moving from each type reveals the two paths one can take, either toward becoming healthier in their type or toward being unhealthy.

For example, a type Three Achiever moving toward health will take on positive aspects of a type Six Loyalist, working for purposes greater than themselves.

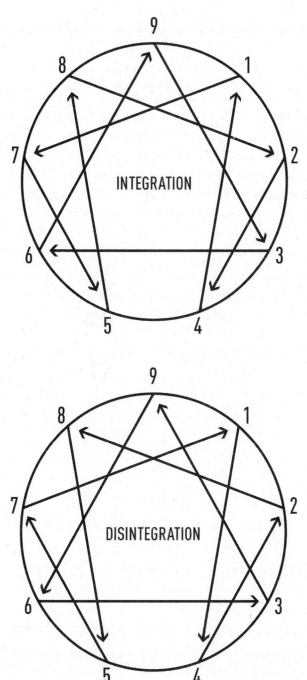

An unhealthy direction for a Three is moving toward type Nine, the Peacemaker. These Threes, usually so keen to achieve, become slothful and give up on their plans and goals, digressing from God's original intent for their lives. They can even lose interest in themselves, and failure becomes devastating.

As we go through each type, we will point out both the paths toward and away from health. The key to becoming healthy in your type is cooperating with the Holy Spirit as He deconstructs the false illusions of who we are and centers us back upon God. As we continue this process, our God-given destiny can be realized as we allow the Holy Spirit to open our eyes to our true self while also giving us a clearer vision of others and their unique gifts.

For our purposes, you will, at best, only get a general overview of the Enneagram from this book. There are many resources available on the Enneagram for those who want to know more. Screen everything you read through the Word of God and allow the Holy Spirit to lead and *"guide you into all the truth"* (John 16:13).

My deepest prayer is that this book will help you dive deeper into God's destiny for you. We are all needed. We all matter. We were all made uniquely in our mother's womb for such a time as this!

4

TYPE ONE – THE REFORMER

Type Ones on the Enneagram are the idealists, the perfectionists, and the reformers. In her book *The Enneagram in Love and Work*, Helen Palmer describes Ones as those who "challenge you to correct action and effort. You can count on them keeping their promises and accepting responsibility to make things right. The buck stops there. They value right action for its own sake without the expectation of benefits. Virtue is its own reward."[6]

Virtue and goodness flow freely from Ones' lives. They are geniuses of perception and can immediately recognize when something is out of place. They have "Spidey senses," a keen ability that extends to all areas of their lives. Ones are rule keepers because failure to do so means leaving something out of order. Ones place a high value on principles, rules, and good ethics. They are bothered when things are not done right, when spaces are disorganized, or there exists what they deem to be sloppiness. They

6. Palmer, *The Enneagram in Love and Work*, 52.

are very dedicated to everything having its correct place, to tasks being properly completed and executed in the right order. This can be taxing to the other Enneagram types, but Ones are extremely important contributors to the success of any team. The devil truly is in the details. Ones' standard of excellence raises the quality and integrity of everything they touch.

When a One is choosing a spouse, they look for possible mates who are clean and orderly. A messy car or house can spell doom for any potential suitors.

While Ones keep themselves busy and are whirlwinds of activity, their inward motivation for constant doing is often hidden from them. Ones stay busy because unmet desires and needs will continue to emerge during downtime. They fill each day with activities to calm their anxious hearts. For Ones, as natural-born critics, the court is always in session. The prosecutor's voice is always going off in their heads, which is exhausting for them. Imagine the inner frustration that builds within a One as they continually disappoint themselves and fail to live up to their own high standards.

ONES ARE HARDER ON THEMSELVES THAN THEY ARE ON ANYBODY AROUND THEM, SIMPLY BECAUSE THEIR OWN PERSONAL FLAWS AND IMPERFECTIONS ARE NAKED AND OPEN TO THEM.

Ones are harder on themselves than they are on anybody around them, simply because their own personal flaws and imperfections are naked and open to them. They have no place to hide. There is no shutting it off! Ones critique themselves beyond what any other Enneagram type can comprehend. Their driving desire to be good, to do things accurately, and to give their very best puts tremendous pressure upon them. Their inner frustration for falling short of perfection can result in communication that comes across as judgmental. The critical way in which they see and communicate is often misunderstood and can drive others away.

If you happen to be the recipient of this inner frustration and feel it being projected upon you, it is helpful to remember that the judgment that Ones display outwardly has already been rendered inwardly. They are their own judge, jury, and court of appeals. It's easier to have compassion and empathy for Ones when we comprehend that, for them, their own imperfections are a glaring reality that they must continually come to grips with every waking moment of every day. They just want to get it right and do good. Keeping everything and everyone in their proper place is exhausting, but it silences the One's inward critic for much-needed reprieves. For these reasons, very few people can keep the pace of a One.

The greatest fear of a One is being bad or corrupt. They fear the criticism of doing things incorrectly and letting others down. Because of this, Ones are known to take on entirely too much responsibility for everyone's work in order to ensure the perfect result they are always seeking.

Ones generally avoid risk because risk leads to mistakes. When in doubt, they will wait. They don't like to take chances. The overwhelming fear of making a wrong decision can paralyze a One. They find it hard to decide on a matter when the outcome holds great weight and usually need others to help them move forward. This is where the power of synergy can really come into play. The due diligence of a One working in concert with a Three or an Eight, who can always make a decision, right or wrong, can be a powerful combination. Such a pair can usually find the correct solution by working together.

In the work environment, Ones reshape abstract approaches into step-by-step procedures. They write everything down using lists and extensive details. At home, it wouldn't be surprising to find their simple grocery list converted to a beautifully laid out spreadsheet.

Ones are always rooting for the underdog in the story. Their deep need for wrongs to be made right motivates them to cheer on those who are crippled by a disadvantage or those who show improvement as a result of raw personal effort.

It's the living things that blossom and grow that make them feel alive. Ones are generally nature lovers. They absorb everything that is the outdoors. Gardening, hiking, trees, and flowers are high on their list of favorites.

> **ONES MUST LEARN TO RECOGNIZE THEIR FIXATION WITH PERFECTION AND REMIND THEMSELVES THAT THIS IS NOT AN IDEAL WORLD.**

Ones must learn to recognize their fixation with perfection and remind themselves that this is not an ideal world. The type One who can step back from seeing all of the imperfections and allow grace to invade their world will find a heart of gratitude more than any other type. They can more deeply grasp the wonder that God loves us unconditionally even in our very broken state. They see grace for what it is—amazing! They have learned to *stop and smell the roses.*

UNHEALTHY ONES

The unhealthy type One who allows their fixation on perfection to consume their every waking moment lives in a constant state of frustration and resentment. It brews under the surface like an active volcano. Left unchecked, these inner passions result in the One's root sin of anger. It's vital that Ones learn to understand themselves so that they can avoid this. If they can acknowledge their ferocious drive to pass judgment on both themselves and others, they can step back and remind themselves that perfection is a process that's difficult, if not impossible, to achieve this side of heaven. It's okay if everything is not perfect today; it seldom will

• be. Ones need to relax, breathe deeply, and remind themselves that there isn't just one correct way to do things.

Without this kind of pause, Ones are prone to project their inner frustrations upon any suitable target around them. Their bottled-up negative emotions must find an escape. Thus, unhealthy Ones will release them on the first person within earshot. They justify their blowup by reasoning that, "They had it coming," or "I've told them a hundred times how to do it right," or "They should have read my list."

Upon introspection, a One moving toward health will acknowledge the part they play in the conflict. By owning their anger, they can spare themselves the guilt that comes from taking their frustrations out upon their children, spouse, or an unsuspecting friend who unfortunately landed in their line of fire.

The unhealthy One can live a very lonely life with few close friends. Their propensity to critique and judge all things can keep others at arm's length. In *The Enneagram: A Journey of Self Discovery*, the authors state that Ones "typically come into a situation with a bias in their thinking, making the situation deal with them instead of trying to understand how all the aspects of the situation fit together. Ones characteristically suffer from a lack of objective perspective in their thinking."[7]

The disapproval of an imperfect world smoldering in an unhealthy One is often evident even without verbal expression. Their bent toward perfectionism raises others' defenses, leaving these Ones often on the outside of social circles. This is extremely painful for an extroverted One.

The rabbit hole can go even deeper if the unhealthy extroverted One falls into the vicious cycle of increased personal judgment upon themselves. They convince themselves that others

---

7. Maria Beesing, Robert J. Nogosek, and Patrick H. O'Leary, *The Enneagram: A Journey of Self Discovery* (Denville, NJ: Dimension Books Inc., 1984), 149.

would invite them to their gatherings if they could just improve their own imperfections. The harder they judge themselves, the more they lean into the trap of judging and critiquing all things.

> **THE ELIXIR OF THE ENNEAGRAM IS THE ABILITY TO IDENTIFY OUR FIXATIONS FOR WHAT THEY ARE AND REMOVE THE LENSES THAT COLOR OUR ENTIRE WORLD.**

The elixir of the Enneagram is the ability to identify our fixations for what they are and remove the lenses that color our entire world. This allows us to see the world as it truly is and forgo judgment upon ourselves and others.

Unhealthy Ones disintegrate toward the Four, the Individualist. These Ones believe the lie that they alone understand and value excellence. They believe the lie that no one else appears to be capable of grasping what is needed to right the ship. Unrealistic standards pile up while their inner frustration grows. They become lost and angry that things don't stay as they should for very long, and thus their idea of perfection is never achieved. For this reason, Ones find it difficult to delegate responsibility because they worry about the job being done correctly. Although rare, whenever they *do* make a mistake, they are prone to shift the blame or quickly point out, "It wasn't my fault." Their deep need to be correct can lead them into needless arguments about who was right.

HEALTHY ONES

Perhaps no other Enneagram type will appreciate heaven more than Ones, who long for a place of perfection and order. God gave us seasons to remind us that all of His creation is in flux. Each season brings with it movement toward His desired end as we inch closer to becoming what He wants us to be. All of creation *"looks forward to the day when it will join God's children in glorious freedom from death and decay"* (Romans 8:21 NLT). This truth has the ability to release Ones from the trap of perfection. A healthy One puts their mind to rest by remembering that we are all in a process of growth, and God's perfection is enough. When Ones daily meditate on the greatness of our God and His perfect plan in place for all of creation, they find serenity and peace.

Healthy Ones still see the imperfections, but their previous fixation on them turns into gratitude as they recognize that God still moves, works, and loves, despite all that is wrong in our world. This allowance makes imperfection acceptable to a One on a visceral level. Their gift to see what is out of order becomes a blessing rather than a curse. Each improvement, though imperfect, is appreciated for its growth toward a desired end. They can silence their own inner critic by reminding themselves that they are also in a process, that God doesn't make junk, and that only through Christ, not our own efforts, can we be brought into perfection.

When God-centered, healthy Ones silence their basic fear of being bad, imbalanced, defective, or corrupt, they are affable people who become both a joy and a great resource to those around them. Their basic desire is to be good and have integrity. Because they have found the grace to silence the prosecutor in their mind, they can easily extend grace to others. Their inner critic morphs into a much-needed traffic cop that can help those around them navigate life better. Healthy Ones cease striving and find rest in the amazing, undeserved grace of Jesus. The peace and goodness they then project are inviting and disarming. The level of integrity they maintain ejects pretense from their lives. These are some of the most genuine and kind people you will ever meet. Their gift becomes a blessing as they apply it where it is welcomed.

Ones want to make things right and will gladly put their shoulders to the work. Simply put, they get things done. If you need something done and done correctly, you need a One on your team. Threes and Eights will confidently declare that they know the correct choice for nearly every decision, but trust the Ones. They have done their due diligence and are always intent on getting it right the first time. They have checked off their list and filled in all of the blanks.

When Ones become more lighthearted, they gravitate toward the enthusiasm of the Enneagram Seven, the Dreamer. A great sense of adventure and optimism invades the heart of a healthy One, and their imagination comes alive with possibilities. Dreams once forgotten are reborn, and Ones become enchanting, fun-loving adventurers.

BIBLICAL EXAMPLE: PAUL

Many identify the apostle Paul as a type One on the Enneagram. His own words implicate him:

> I was circumcised when I was eight days old. I am a pure-blooded citizen of Israel and a member of the tribe of Benjamin—a real Hebrew if there ever was one! I was a member of the Pharisees, who demand the strictest obedience to the Jewish law. I was so zealous that I harshly persecuted the church. And as for righteousness, I obeyed the law without fault. I once thought these things were valuable, but now I consider them worthless because of what Christ has done.
> (Philippians 3:5–7 NLT)

Paul had dotted all the I's and crossed all his T's. This perfect Pharisee was so convinced of his righteousness that he was willing to murder those who were disrupting his perfect world. From his own skewed perspective, Paul needed to set things right. This is the true danger of being self-deceived: we believe a lie and then act accordingly.

Thankfully, Paul was not left to himself and his root sin of anger. A personal encounter with Jesus changed everything! (See

Acts 9:1–22.) We see Paul's transformation toward health immediately. With the same zeal that was formerly misguided, the redeemed apostle outperforms all of his contemporaries for the cause of Christ.

We see the type One in Paul through his careful instructions to the churches in the Epistles. His letters are concise, taking nothing for granted. It is easy to see Paul's attention to detail in his instructions to his understudy Timothy.

When things were imperfect, Paul confronted Peter—one of the three disciples closest to Jesus—to his face and in front of everyone:

> *But when Peter came to Antioch, I had to oppose him to his face, for what he did was very wrong. When he first arrived, he ate with the Gentile believers, who were not circumcised. But afterward, when some friends of James came, Peter wouldn't eat with the Gentiles anymore. He was afraid of criticism from these people who insisted on the necessity of circumcision. As a result, other Jewish believers followed Peter's hypocrisy, and even Barnabas was led astray by their hypocrisy. When I saw that they were not following the truth of the gospel message, I said to Peter in front of all the others, "Since you, a Jew by birth, have discarded the Jewish laws and are living like a Gentile, why are you now trying to make these Gentiles follow the Jewish traditions?*   (Galatians 2:11–14 NLT)

From this exchange, we see a type One who knew he was correct and didn't back down, even for Peter. Paul was right to do what he did. God used his gift to bring the correction that was needed.

PAUL'S LIFE STORY GIVES A DETAILED LOOK INTO BOTH A HEALTHY AND AN UNHEALTHY ONE. A PERSONAL RELATIONSHIP WITH JESUS MADE ALL OF THE DIFFERENCE.

Paul's life story gives a detailed look into both a healthy and an unhealthy One. A personal relationship with Jesus made all the difference.

Paul's story can be ours. We are all broken people in desperate need of our Savior. We can all invite Jesus and the Holy Spirit to guide us into truth and wholeness.

Jesus exemplified healthy and whole versions of all nine Enneagram types. We don't have to search very hard to see Jesus as the Reformer. He left His throne in heaven and came to earth to be born in a lowly manger because the world was not as it was intended. Jesus came to set things in order and show us the way forward. He said, *"You therefore must be perfect, as your heavenly Father is perfect"* (Matthew 5:48 ESV). Jesus gave us a living example of what this looks like by His words and His actions. He was able to say of Himself, *"I have not spoken on my own authority, but the Father who sent me has himself given me a commandment—what to say and what to speak"* (John 12:49 ESV) Even His words were perfect. His communication with those in error was direct and open. He exposed deception and brought hidden motives to light. Jesus was clearly on a mission to right all that is wrong in the world.

A MOTHER'S TESTIMONY

Here is the personal testimony of a type One, a middle-aged mother with two children. Her prayer life changed after she learned about the Enneagram.

—

I find that the Enneagram is extremely helpful on many levels. It helps you to understand yourself and those in your life. I am a One wing Two. The One is the perfectionist. Now that I am aware of that, I try not to be so hard on myself. Ones can be busy trying to make the world a perfect place, which we all know is impossible. My to-do lists are endless, but I know I don't have to get it all done *now*. Tomorrow is a new day! I will catch myself saying, "You're just being a perfectionist. Lighten up a little." I also try not to expect others to do things "perfectly" either. This mindset is helpful in all of your relationships—spouses, children, siblings, friendships, and everyone in between. I understand that they are operating out of the hardwired personality that God gave *them*. It gives you more grace and understanding for others. Of course, it is not an excuse for unhealthy behavior or not doing what you need to do. It is a great tool, though. This may sound odd, but I believe it helps with your prayers as well. If you know someone's strengths and weaknesses, you can target your prayers a little more specifically. It comes in handy when you pray for your kids and as you help guide them with their decisions. It can help them pick a good job that suits them well, or a spouse who is a good match. They can find someone who is strong where they are weak and vice versa. I would have to say that there is not a day that I don't employ the Enneagram in my life.

5

TYPE TWO – THE HELPER

One of the most gracious and generous of all the Enneagram types is the Two, known as the Helper. Their deepest desire is to give and receive love. Twos will give all that they are, and all they possess, in the most perfect ways. They will be the most caring and considerate friends you will ever have. Twos are often seen frantically dashing about, being as helpful as possible so that the people in their lives feel nurtured. The time, energy, and resources they pour into others make Twos amazing companions.

> A TWO'S GREATEST NEED IS TO BE NEEDED. THEY PRIDE THEMSELVES ON BEING HELPFUL, ESPECIALLY TO THOSE NEAR AND DEAR TO THEM.

A Two's greatest need is to be needed. Nearly every Two will immediately recognize this as their deepest heartfelt desire. They pride themselves on being helpful, especially to those near and dear to them. They consider themselves to be good when they are loving, selfless, and helpful. You will find that many Twos support the less fortunate in developing countries, especially children.

When healthy, these people-pleasers contribute a great deal to their communities, but if they are brutally honest with themselves, they will admit that they frequently do so in order to receive the same kind of tender affection that they themselves provide. This is because the greatest fear of a Two is to be unloved, to be valued only for what they give and not who they are. No one desires love as much as a Two.

Getting a Two to tell you what they really want can cause them tremendous stress. They avoid recognizing that they have their own needs. My daughter is a Two, and even on her birthdays, when asked what restaurant or what activity she would enjoy, she would try to defer to what everyone else preferred. It caused her great stress to acknowledge her own preference because she wanted to make sure our desires were met first.

Twos frequently feel guilty about making a decision based upon their own wants, and asking for their own needs to be met can fill a Two with a deep sense of shame. Simply acknowledging their needs can trigger the same painful effect. The vicious cycle these Helpers can fall into is that they secretly expect others to reciprocate everything they've received from the Two. When this doesn't happen, the Two is not only disappointed, but also ashamed for expecting their needs to be met.

When healthy, Twos learn to give love unconditionally to others and, most importantly, to themselves as well. They learn to voice their own needs and reach out to friends and family. When a type Two experiences this kind of growth, they can appreciate the unconditional and generous love that Jesus gives.

Twos become healthy by moving toward an Enneagram type Four, the Individualist. By intentionally seeing themselves as unique individuals with their own set of feelings and needs, the healthy Twos free themselves from being cast aside as mere Helpers without any needs of their own. Healthy Twos can acknowledge their own deep need to be appreciated for being kind, sensitive individuals rather than for their service to others. They really are unique in their special ability to show an immense amount of love for others in the most fitting of ways.

UNHEALTHY TWOS

Abandoning individuality, unhealthy Twos starve themselves of their own needs while at the same time becoming overly involved in the lives of others. An unhealthy Two allows their need to be needed to drive their decision-making. Convincing themselves that they are happy to see others content, they genuinely believe that this is all they *need* to be satisfied. If unhealthy Twos honestly examine their lives, they quickly realize that they have no hobbies, interests, or passions independent of others. This lifestyle allows both pride and resentment to creep in, feeding into their discontent.

> UNHEALTHY TWOS BECOME PRIDEFUL AND DECEIVED INTO BELIEVING THAT NO ONE CARES ENOUGH OR DOES AS MUCH AS THEY DO.

Unhealthy Twos become prideful and deceived into believing that no one cares enough or does as much as they do. The root sin of a Two is their pride, which is not expressed as conceit or narcissism but rather in the form of an inflated ego. These Twos see themselves as more loving and caring than anyone else around them, and they strive to prove that this is true, that no one can give as much as they can. They believe that they are so sensitive and tuned into the needs of others that, without them, their loved ones' lives would fall apart. Their unhealthy perception can cause these Twos to act like they're the world's saviors. Twos are fixated on flattery, possessing a desperate need for validation. Can you imagine the pressure?

Their resentment brews when they see themselves as invaluable to the *team*, yet hate the fact that no one takes care of *their* needs—needs that the Twos have never voiced, so others don't even know what they are. Harboring this resentment, Twos silently stew over all of their hard work that is never fully appreciated. This eventually leads to an ugly explosion, followed by a tearful apology and shame. Then, the cycle repeats itself.

And yet Twos must remain ever vigilant, for it's easy for others to take advantage of their good-natured generosity. They will give and give of themselves until there is nothing left to contribute. Even when they know deep down that they are *being played*, Twos can quickly shame themselves for having needs of their own and readily discount the misuse. When friends or family accurately point it out, the Two will generally acknowledge it…but immediately allow it to continue.

In *The Enneagram: A Christian Perspective*, Richard Rohr and Andreas Ebert point out:

> All you have to say to a Two is "I need you," and all resistance fades. They fall all over you to be useful to you and to help you—even when they have neither the time nor the energy to do it. As soon as they hear the little word "need," they scrape together the last remnant of their energy to rush to help you. Later, they go home and kick themselves for letting themselves be talked into it: "Why did I let myself be exploited again?"[8]

For this reason, unhealthy Twos need other healthy types around them for their own protection and well-being.

Sadly, an average to unhealthy Two can spend their entire life in the shadow of another and never fully realize their own God-given uniqueness and destiny. Many Twos in this unhealthy situation divorce their spouses late into a marriage as their silent

8. Rohr and Ebert, *The Enneagram: A Christian Perspective*, 65.

resentment grows. As they mature, they conclude, "I have no life of my own," and tragically see divorce as their only option. They believe that the only way forward is to separate themselves from the one who has cast a lifelong shadow over them. This is a mistake of enormous proportions. The real answer is to grow in health by integrating the positive aspects of type Four, the Individualist. The Two's spouse must be willing to give them the room, permission, and support to do so.

As a dangerous side effect, comfort food can become a real temptation for unhealthy Twos. When the same love and attention they gave to others is not reciprocated, they can easily return home from all of their bustling activity of serving others and justify why they have *earned* the chocolate pie, potato chips, or tub of ice cream. For this reason, many Twos experience weight challenges. They compensate with comfort food for the imbalance they feel when the amount of love and care they have given is not reciprocated.

HEALTHY TWOS

By being willing to identify and fulfill their own needs, healthy Twos put themselves in a position to give from a place of overflow rather than emptiness. They assert themselves, find their true selves, and set parameters for their own needs. Everyone benefits as a result. Healthy Twos' newly discovered autonomy frees them to become the people God intended them to be. They no longer need their worth to be continually reinforced by taking care of others, for they have found their identity in Christ.

HEALTHY TWOS ASSERT THEMSELVES AND SET PARAMETERS FOR THEIR OWN NEEDS. THEY NO LONGER NEED THEIR WORTH TO BE CONTINUALLY REINFORCED BY TAKING CARE OF OTHERS.

A peacefully redeemed Two puts their mind to rest by focusing on the fact that God is their most significant source of love. The most humbling thought of a Two is acutely knowing that Jesus's passion led Him to the cross and realizing that He would do it all over again *just for them*. None of us have earned His love; He gave it freely with no strings attached. This realization is both heartbreaking and liberating for a Two. It allows them to give up their desperate drive to earn endearment and makes room for unconditional tenderness toward both others and themselves. The gift of the redeemed Two is humility.

When healthy, this type recognizes the honor it is to love and be loved. They realize the privilege of taking part in another's life, and they learn to respect others' boundaries. Healthy Twos can happily serve others in ways that go unnoticed or unrewarded.

Healthy Twos are a joy in the workplace and are experts at making others look good. They are happy to show unconditional support from behind the scenes. In the area of outreach and promotion, healthy Twos excel. They represent others well and protect the interests of their employers faithfully.

You can count on Twos to know and be known by everyone. They are experts at rallying teamwork because they have proven to be loyal friends who will jump in and assist others anytime there is a need. Twos make extraordinary team players because they are always ready to help, mindful of everyone's feelings, and full of valuable suggestions.

Twos put their energy into their work and stay attuned to the dynamics of the organization. They are extremely aware of how everyone is doing and strive to remedy and reunite everyone to a working harmony. No one can keep you better informed of how the team is doing than a healthy Two.

Twos love you with their whole being, and they see you for who you are, flaws and all. The healthy Two is profoundly unselfish, deeply humble, and genuinely helpful. They will give you the shirt off their back and always be there for you.

When the chips are down, the Two will be the one present for others in their hour of need. Even complete strangers are able to sense how attuned they are to the needs of others and will quickly pour their hearts out to them.

BIBLICAL EXAMPLE: JOHN THE BELOVED

The apostle John was most likely an Enneagram type Two. He was known for open displays of affection for Jesus. Peter, John, and John's brother James were closest to Jesus and saw the Lord do things that the other apostles did not, such as raising Jairus's daughter from the dead. (See Mark 5:37.)

John also demonstrated the characteristics of a Two in Jesus's final moments. As Jesus hung on the cross, *"the disciple whom he loved"* (John 19:26) was literally the only man still standing. Knowing John's heart, Jesus knew He could entrust His mother to John's care and so said, *"'Woman, here is your son,' and to the disciple, 'Here is your mother.' From that time on, this disciple took her into his home"* (John 19:26–27). Jesus knew from His own personal experience that John would love and care for Mary as his own mother. This is the power of a healthy Two.

A YOUNG WOMAN'S TESTIMONY

Here is the personal testimony of a twenty-five-year-old woman from Florida who is a type Two. She explains the value she found in learning to say *no*.

Before discovering the Enneagram, I'd say that I was a typical Two. If a friend was moving, I would help them pack, move, unpack…and I'd probably bring snacks for the group. ;) My life was consumed with meeting others' needs, be it a close friend or perfect stranger. Anyone who *needed* me had my full attention and energy. Life was a game of, "How can I fit your need into my schedule?" and I was going to win, even if I was harmed in the process. *No* was not a word in my vocabulary. It might as well have been in a foreign language.

Then came the Enneagram. Ouch! LOL!

I quickly discovered that all of this *good* I had been doing wasn't as selfless as it appeared to be. I wasn't helping out of the goodness of my heart. I was quenching a never-ending *need to be needed*. Humiliated and heartbroken by this realization, I was determined to break loose from this unhealthy mentality. So, I changed my life—my mental life, that is. From that moment on, every decision and action was run through the filter of, "*Why* am I doing this?" I was constantly asking myself, "Am I doing this because I genuinely think it will be a blessing to this person, or am I doing this for me?" Then, if it was for the other person, no strings attached, I'd move forward. If not, I wouldn't take any further action.

If you are a Two, you realize how life-altering this idea is!

After a full year of changing my decision-making process, I began to uncover more truths about myself through the Enneagram. For example, I have needs. Shocking, I know. Even writing that statement makes me uncomfortable, but it's true. The only way to become a healthy Two is to work through the shame of having those needs and to share them with others. Truthfully, this is a lesson that I am still working on.

The other day, I decided to take a baby step in the right direction. Sitting at the dinner table, I realized that I needed the ranch dressing, which was far out of my reach and directly next to my boyfriend's hand. Instead of doing my usual ninja move where I reach as far as humanly possible and potentially sprain a muscle, I decided it was time to express my need. And I *needed* the ranch. So, I politely asked for the dressing, and he graciously obliged. For the next *thirty minutes*, I was consumed with guilt. I lost my appetite. Finally, I confessed that I felt guilty about asking for the ranch dressing when I could have just grabbed it myself. To which he responded, "That was no problem! Honestly, I don't even remember passing you the ranch."

My point is this: your needs are only a big deal to *you*. Others aren't shocked by them. In fact, they expect you to have them. Do you know why? Because *you are human*. Ask for the ranch. Have a need or two. It'll be okay, and you'll be better for it.

My final discovery was the most liberating yet heartbreaking. It's a simple concept but a hard lesson. I can't save everyone. I can't *will* someone to be okay. They are not my responsibility, and I can't make the *right decision* for them. Wow. The minute you truly let go of this responsibility that wasn't yours in the first place, you will find peace. Only then will you be able to love others without trying to control them.

6

TYPE THREE – THE ACHIEVER

The worldview of an Enneagram Three is that you *must* win in life. For this type, known as the Achiever, failure is not an option. They are driven by the need to succeed. This competitive nature is fueled by an internal need to prove to themselves that they are valuable.

Threes are keenly aware and always engaged in building their brand. Always aware of their image, Threes are usually attractive people and choose highly attractive spouses. Frequently, they choose marketing, public speaking, acting, or sales for their careers. They are born actors.

While others will wait to fill in all the blanks, Threes have no problem with winging it and jumping right in. Activity is believed to be favorable to learning. Mistakes are simply seen as falling forward rather than failing. Threes will raise their hands to answer a question even if they don't know the answer because they learn as they go. Not inclined to hold back, Threes grow impatient with delays due to a long-winded theory, or what they view as mere details.

Few other types can fully understand the jet engine of ambition that is always ignited in a Three. It is always driving, always reaching for the next best thing. For them, the upcoming project is always lurking just around the corner. The internal drive of this type can be both a blessing and a curse. It never sleeps. To be healthy, Threes must learn when to bring their ambitions under submission to Christ. This does not mean they need to become idle. In fact, inactivity is unhealthy for a Three, for they find reasons to hope and live through meaningful achievements.

Threes are natural-born leaders who have the ability to motivate others to action. Above all else, Threes inspire us. Encouraging and enthusiastic, they have the ability to read others to determine what will inspire them to join their cause. Their optimism believes, "We can make it happen if we try."

> **THE THREE'S ABILITY TO BE ATTUNED TO OTHERS IS IRONIC BECAUSE NO OTHER ENNEAGRAM TYPE IS MORE UNAWARE OF THEIR OWN FEELINGS.**

The Three's ability to be attuned to others is ironic because no other Enneagram type is more *unaware* of their own feelings. Commonly, when asked, "How does that make you feel?" a Three will stare blankly back with no answer. They simply are so pragmatic about achieving that they never really consider the answer. It's not important. Their own feelings are dismissed as inefficient emotions that serve no purpose; the current goal is the thing. Threes must work hard to become aware of their own feelings because they often consider their personal emotions as cumbersome extra baggage that is simply too hard to carry on life's journey. If the job or project demands it, they will simply leave their emotions behind because, above all else, a Three needs to win.

When in a crowd, Threes thrive, but they often seem disconnected or aloof to others. They wish to keep enough distance to properly lead and relate to those they intend to guide without revealing too much of themselves. They often conclude that too much excessive personal information could only hinder the mission at hand.

Threes and Eights (the Challenger) are often mistaken for one another, and for the most part, there's a mutual appreciation and admiration. They can make a marvelous team if the primary tension between both types is resolved. This tension involves the Three's need to have some measure of autonomy and the Eight's need for power and control. Threes must feel free, without restraints, in some areas of their responsibilities, or they begin to feel trapped. Eights who are too immature or unhealthy to allow for this autonomy will quickly drive the Three away. This is a real loss because there's great synergy when a Three and an Eight are on the same team.

The Three's ability to move a crowd toward achievement can cause the unhealthy Three to overlook the individual. One-on-one time is simply viewed as inefficient. When working toward a goal, Threes become stingy with their time because they know the energy spent on one individual could be better spent moving the masses. Also, Threes in one-on-one conversations find it hard to express their own feelings on a matter since they've disconnected from their emotions. All such exchanges leave the Three feeling vulnerable or exposed to *a stranger*, even though they may have casually known the other person for years. In those moments, they think, *How can I share my personal feelings with you when I don't even know them myself?* Their struggle to come to grips with their own authentic emotions is highly personal, and they can only share their feelings with those they know intimately—their spouses, close friends, and family members. Otherwise, they feel vulnerable, which is both a threat to building their brand and a deterrent to quickly and efficiently achieving the task at hand.

Work levels that most find stressful are welcomed by Threes. They feel in control when there's something constructive to do. Their free time is often accompanied by an anxiety that moves them quickly on to the next project. They seemingly have no ability to relax the need to win. They are naturally competitive and will give it their all when stated goals are well defined, with clear rewards if reached. Give them opportunities for advancement, and they will soar. Conversely, if you want to make a Three feel uncomfortable, give them what they consider to be unwarranted praise or rewards.

HIGHLY PRAGMATIC, THREES ONLY READ LINE ITEMS ON FINANCIAL REPORTS WHEN THEY DEEM THEM NECESSARY; THEIR EYES GO IMMEDIATELY TO THE BOTTOM LINE.

Highly pragmatic, Threes only read line items on financial reports when they deem them necessary; their eyes go immediately to the bottom line. When trying to get answers from team members, they can often become impatient with what they view as rambling. When answering a Three, the best approach is to give them the bottom line first and then fill in all the details if asked.

As I mentioned earlier, people often confuse Threes for Eights and vice versa because in many situations, they operate in a similar manner. I have found that one of the best ways to determine between the types is to note their regard for details. While a Three will go directly to the bottom line in a report and just want "important" details, an Eight will absorb all of the line items, not only demanding exact details, but also giving the same great attention to the bottom line that the Three will display. I call this the *report test*. If you are trying to determine whether someone is a Three or an Eight, this characteristic will prove most revealing.

UNHEALTHY THREES

When they are unhealthy, the Three will be chameleon-like, taking on whatever role is needed to move those in front of them toward their cause. Because Threes are so separated from their own feelings, they can change their views on an issue without any internal turmoil for their hypocrisy. This is a dangerous game because it is easy for them to lose their true self along the way. Not surprisingly, many politicians are Threes. Their stance on an issue can change depending on their audience. Their prominent need to succeed deceives them into believing that the end justifies the means. The root sin of a Three is deceit, although their lies are not as diabolical as some believe.

The self-identifying lie that the Three must avoid is, "I am what I do." Seeking affirmation, Threes will take on other roles to gain admiration, appreciation, and value. This external affirmation helps to convince them of their worth and fills their barren souls with much-needed feelings of love.

The basic fear of this type is to be worthless, so they avoid failure at all costs. Failure is the term that describes Three's avoidance. There is nothing more tragic than an unsuccessful Three because of the trauma it causes them when dealing with defeat. Threes simply hate to lose.

Unhealthy Threes have three standard ways of removing themselves from failure:

1. They put as much distance as possible between themselves and the loss by becoming fully engaged in the next interesting or promising venture.

2. They spin the loss as a partial victory with some unexpected positive outcome.

3. They shift the blame to someone else—"I'm not the problem!"

When a defeat is so great that they cannot see a way to extricate themselves from it, unhealthy Threes frequently view suicide as their only option.

Judas Iscariot demonstrated an unhealthy Three's characteristics when his thirst for achievement led him to betray Jesus for thirty pieces of silver. While the other disciples called Jesus "Lord," Judas called Him "rabbi," meaning teacher or mentor. Judas was deceitful and greedy, complaining when Mary of Bethany anointed Jesus, *"'Why wasn't this perfume sold and the money given to the poor? It was worth a year's wages.' He did not say this because he cared about the poor but because he was a thief; as keeper of the money bag, he used to help himself to what was put into it"* (John 12:5–6).

Judas made his decision to betray Christ after Jesus made it clear that He intended to give His life for the cause of redemption. Judas viewed this as defeat and moved quickly to extricate himself from it. He reasoned he would turn this disaster into a partial victory by receiving payment for his betrayal and shifted the blame to Jesus for His foolhardiness. When Judas realized his gigantic miscalculation, he viewed death as his only option and tragically took his own life.

HEALTHY THREES

Healthy Threes have a gift for honesty or truthfulness, a reverse of their root sin of deceit. Quieting their need for affirmation and validation, they refuse to be actors who are disconnected from their true selves; instead, they share their genuine thoughts, feelings, and opinions with others.

In relationships, Threes need assurances that they are loved for who they are and not for their achievements. Their natural drive for success will need to be tempered by a loving mate who can hold them accountable, encourage them to take time away from work, and help them celebrate the marginal victories, not just the big ones.

Healthy Threes can be critical of their own tendencies to air-brush their imperfections and shortcomings. They strive for integrity in all things and willingly admit when they have stretched the truth to polish the mask. When a Three can learn to fail and embrace failure as *falling forward*, they can begin to be truthful first with themselves and then with others.

Redeemed Threes see the value of the individual and pause the efficiency button that would cause them to overlook their needs. Face-to-face exchanges are then not viewed as energy wasted.

REDEEMED THREES USE THEIR CHARM AND INFLUENCE TO INSPIRE HOPE IN A WORLD THAT POSSESSES FAR TOO LITTLE OF IT.

These Threes use their charm and influence to inspire hope in a world that possesses far too little of it. Their generous smiles and warm hearts bring people together for the greater good while they defer the credit to the team rather than seeking affirmation for themselves. They stop building their own kingdom and start building Christ's.

To be healthy, Threes must constantly examine their personal motives for achievement. They must quiet themselves to get in touch with their own feelings and stop dismissing them. They need to embrace solitude, step away from the crowds and the applause, and stop relying on others for validation.

Redeemed Threes embrace the failure of the cross by understanding that God makes His own greatest victories out of what most view as our failures. Redeemed Threes can move mountains and do mighty exploits for God.

Some have identified the rich young man who came to Jesus in Mark 10:17–27 as a type Three on the Enneagram. They maintain that when he asked Jesus, *"What must I do to inherit eternal life?"* (verse 17), he was really saying, "I have won in this life; now tell me how to win in the next." If this was the young man's motivation, I would certainly agree that he demonstrated the actions of a Three, but I would avoid labeling him, or anyone else for that matter, from one life event. Although this was surely the most significant exchange of his entire life, we cannot know from this brief conversation whether he was a type Three.

For example, it's possible that this man was a Five, the Investigator, who could have been watching Jesus from afar, waiting to seize the opportunity to go to Jesus for answers. When Jesus told him, *"Go, sell everything you have and give to the poor, and you will have treasure in heaven. Then come, follow me"* (Mark 10:21), the price was too high. *"He went away sad, because he had great wealth"* (verse 22).

BIBLICAL EXAMPLE: JACOB

I think the story of Jacob—recorded from his birth all the way to his death—gives us a much better biblical example of a Three. We first find Jacob in Genesis 25:19, and he *"breathed his last"* in Genesis 49:33. So much of his life is disclosed that he is perhaps the most documented biblical character that we can confidently identify on the Enneagram.

Jacob was the quintessential Three—so much so that he struggled with his twin brother Esau to succeed even before his birth. Esau was firstborn, but Jacob was holding onto his older brother's heel as if trying to pull Esau back so that he could arrive first and receive all the honors that come with that distinction. Jacob had to win!

Jacob exemplifies the qualities of an unredeemed Three; he was a deceiver who did whatever it took to succeed. He took advantage of his brother Esau by catching him in a vulnerable moment and bought his brother's birthright for a mere bowl of stew. (See Genesis 25:29–34.) He used his charm to win his mother's favoritism and then went along with her plan to trick his dying elderly blind father. Together they carried out an elaborate plan for Jacob to triumph over Esau yet again. (See Genesis 27:1–30.) For Jacob, the end always justified the means.

When fleeing from Esau, Jacob dreamt of a ladder reaching to heaven. I love that God knows how to get our attention. Representing higher success, the ladder is something with which every Three can identify. In this divine encounter, Jacob reveals his *prominent need* to achieve by daring to bargain even with God:

> *Early the next morning Jacob took the stone he had placed under his head and set it up as a pillar and poured oil on top of it. He called that place Bethel, though the city used to be called Luz. Then Jacob made a vow, saying, "If God will be with me and will watch over me on this journey I am taking and will give me food to eat and clothes to wear so that I return safely to my father's household, then the LORD will be my God and this stone that I have set up as a pillar will be God's house, and of all that you give me I will give you a tenth."*
>
> (Genesis 28:18–22)

Jacob soon meets his match in Laban—possibly a type Eight, the Challenger—but Jacob is undeterred, demonstrating the "whatever it takes to achieve" attitude found in Threes. When he is tricked by Laban and given Leah to wed after working seven long years for Rachel, without hesitation, Jacob agrees to work an additional seven years for the younger sister he loves. In the end, Jacob finally breaks from Laban, emerging as the winner.

Jacob's need to succeed took on new heights when he dared to wrestle with God's messenger. (See Genesis 32:24–32.) His motivation was clear when he said, *"Bless me."* What he meant was, "I *have* to win, so bless me!"

JACOB'S NEED TO SUCCEED TOOK ON NEW HEIGHTS WHEN HE DARED TO WRESTLE WITH THE ANGEL, AN ENCOUNTER THAT LEFT HIM GENEROUS AND HUMBLE BEFORE HIS BROTHER ESAU.

But something happened to Jacob during his encounter that needs to occur for every Three to become healthy. Jacob walked away from that wrestling match with a limp, with brokenness. For the rest of his life, Jacob's limp was evident to all. A regenerated Jacob is shown to be both generous and humble before his brother Esau:

> *He himself went on ahead and bowed down to the ground seven times as he approached his brother. But Esau ran to meet Jacob and embraced him; he threw his arms around his neck and kissed him. And they wept. Then Esau looked up and saw the women and children. "Who are these with you?" he asked. Jacob answered, "They are the children God has graciously given your servant." Then the female servants and their children approached and bowed down. Next, Leah and her children came and bowed down. Last of all came Joseph and Rachel, and they too bowed down. Esau asked, "What's the meaning of all these flocks and herds I met?" "To find favor in your eyes, my lord," he said. But Esau said, "I already have plenty, my brother. Keep what you have for yourself." "No, please!" said Jacob. "If I have found favor in your eyes, accept this gift from me. For to see your face is like seeing the face of God, now that you have received me favorably. Please accept the present that was brought to you, for God has been gracious to me and I have all I need." And because Jacob insisted, Esau accepted it.* (Genesis 33:3–11)

As Jacob did with Esau, Threes move to health when they integrate toward type Six, the Loyalist. Less focused on themselves and more considerate of the well-being of those around them, healthy Threes work toward the success and needs of others. Jacob's transformation was immediately witnessed in his generosity to his brother Esau. Jacob began to experience a new way of living. He was so changed by his encounter with God that his transformation came complete with a new name: Israel. Like Dorothy, Jacob found his way home.

Only in Christ can we become all we were meant to be. He moves us from being "me-centered" to "God-centered." A God-centered Three demonstrates authenticity with sincere warmth, integrity, and genuine concern for others. Their accomplishments contribute beauty and significance to our world, bringing glory to God.

AN ACHIEVER'S TESTIMONY

Here is the personal testimony of a man, age forty-one, who has found that learning what it means to be a type Three can help in all facets of life.

Over the years, I have taken several different personality tests, which were very helpful in understanding how other people think and react and helping me understand myself. However, the Enneagram has been the most in-depth and comprehensive test I have taken. It has been a game changer in how I live my Christian walk.

I am a Three (the Achiever) on the Enneagram, which has many positive traits, but many blind spots or growth areas. As Achievers, we have what I like to call "the idea of the day." If you're married to a Three, you understand this. However, sometimes we have to reign in the ideas and know that we can't act on every great idea of the day. I also have come to understand that as a Three, you aren't going to achieve everything you set out to do today, which can lead to frustration, disappointment, and depression if not kept in check. The Enneagram has been a reminder of how God chooses to need each of us working together. He doesn't need us, but He chooses to need us to be a part of the body, and our personality is a part of how He created us. Ecclesiastes 4:4 is a sobering reminder. It says, *"And I saw that all toil and all achievement spring from one person's envy of another. This too is meaningless, a chasing after the wind."* That doesn't mean we can't be the Achievers God called us to be, but it can't replace the God-shaped hole in our hearts.

The Enneagram has also helped me to be the best Achiever possible, not hiding the light that God has given me and enabling me to be the best follower of Christ, husband, daddy, and friend possible. This tool is super helpful in understanding your spouse, children, and team. Whether you're a leader on the team or a part of the team, you will interact with people with different personalities. So, we need to understand what motivates people and what discourages them. I have a long way to go on this journey, but I am so grateful that God has opened my eyes to understanding others and myself.

7

TYPE FOUR – THE INDIVIDUALIST

Type Four on the Enneagram is known as the Individualist. Often skilled artistically, with a natural eye for beauty and exquisite taste, Fours may become poets, painters, artists, dancers, authors, composers, playwrights, musicians, and actors. The entertainment industry is full of Fours.

Fours want to be *different*. Anything that's commonplace or routine is distasteful to them and cannot fill their desire to create. What is current, conventional, or normal would only be described by them as boring. Because they fear becoming just another number, or just another face in the crowd, Fours refuse to conform. When encouraged to "fit in," they push back. The truth is, they don't want to be like everyone else. Whether true or not, they see themselves as *different*, and when that projection is threatened, they will work even harder to set themselves apart from what they perceive to be the norm, sometimes even taking it to the extreme.

Fours work hard to stand out by their appearance, and the irony is that their *look* is pretty much the norm for all Individualists, which makes it quite easy to identify them. These are the artistic types whose combinations of attire prove to be as unique as they are. They often purchase their clothes in secondhand shops, thrift stores, or exotic designer racks. Many Fours will spend a lot of time contemplating and assembling their outfits for just the right look and later claim, "I just threw something on." In their effort to stand out, Fours will fight the status quo. They generally believe that rules don't apply to them. After all, they are *special*!

> IN THEIR EFFORT TO STAND OUT, FOURS WILL FIGHT THE STATUS QUO. THEY GENERALLY BELIEVE THAT RULES DON'T APPLY TO THEM. AFTER ALL, THEY ARE SPECIAL!

Not surprisingly, the attribute of God that is most appreciated by Fours is His originality. They admire this aspect of God because of their own need to be special or unique. When two Fours meet for the first time, there's an instant connection and understanding between them.

While growing up, most Fours felt *different*. As a result, they turned inward to their imagination or feelings. They learned to embrace the pain of isolation almost as a security blanket—the melancholy longing for acceptance. If not guided, this longing can become their closest friend, their way of coping with a distant world that doesn't understand them, whether this perception is valid or not.

Fours are the Enneagram type most aware of their own feelings. Their lifelong emotional calisthenics fine-tunes them to their own emotions, which equips them to understand others' feelings as well. They can often be heard saying, "I know exactly how you feel." Though impossible for anyone to know another's specific pain or joy, of all the types, Fours are the most capable of doing so.

Fours love to mourn what could have been and what could be. Their worldview is, "Somehow, I have missed out," or "What others have attained has somehow escaped my grasp." Fours rehearse the tragedies of their lives repeatedly. They find sweet sadness or melancholy in their perception of loss. In their book *The Enneagram: A Journey of Self Discovery*, Maria Beesing, Robert J. Nogosek, and Patrick H. O'Leary write, "The drama of their lives, especially its sad parts, is viewed as very significant. They feel special because they have been overlooked or abandoned by others or simply not appreciated."[9]

For a Four, nobody knows the trouble they've seen. No one feels the pain they feel. They are hypersensitive to their hurts or misfortunes. The pitfall for Fours is their melancholy approach to life.

Known as tragic romantics, Fours tend to idolize the past, making it far more glorious than it was, while simultaneously dramatizing a future that is impossibly ideal.

Fours often fixate on death as an appealing endgame. In artistic expression, Fours will demonstrate this by including symbols of death in their work: a dead rose, a morbid face, a broken glass mirror, or a macabre scene. Many have an affinity with death and place it on a pedestal.

Whether in the workplace or at home, Fours want to be understood. They want to know that their feelings matter. Fours need great listeners in their lives. They don't need to always have things go their way, but their opinion *must* be heard. Driven by a deep desire to be understood and known, Fours can be guilty of oversharing their feelings and pain. They tend to believe that the uniqueness of what they experienced and the depth of their sorrow make it impossible for anyone else to understand them. Such thoughts cause them to overshare their emotions.

---

9. Beesing, et al., *The Enneagram: A Journey of Self Discovery*, 69.

Their search for significance is endless and always active, but this inner drive causes them to find beauty in all things. Many artists, poets, and songwriters are Fours. Details often overlooked by others will catch the eye of the Four, allowing them to find treasures that no one else can see. When unhealthy, their unique ability to see beauty in all things is sadly wasted on themselves as they wallow in their melancholy state. Their eye for detail, unfortunately, highlights their own flaws, which leads them to believe that their flaws prevent them from fitting in.

The great effort Fours exert to stand out often causes others to judge them as attention-seekers. This drive to be noticed can easily be misunderstood because the Four's own motivation for distinction is frequently a mystery even to themselves. Through their attire, outlandish remarks, and any other means necessary, this type wants to be seen because they quietly hope that others can tell them who they really are. Fours seek for others to identify and affirm them, even though, deep down, they secretly believe that no one really can. After all, Fours think, *How could they? I'm far too unique to be understood.* This quest for affirmation makes being noticed of critical importance.

> FOURS SEEK FOR OTHERS TO IDENTIFY AND AFFIRM THEM,
> EVEN THOUGH, DEEP DOWN,
> THEY SECRETLY BELIEVE THAT NO ONE REALLY CAN.

UNHEALTHY FOURS

The Four's greatest fear is having no identity or significance. They often feel lost in the crowd, with no real personal importance or substance. The real irony here is that other Enneagram types generally consider Fours to be uniquely interesting people.

The unhealthy Four acts out of the envious belief that "others enjoy life while I am deprived." In *The Enneagram in Love and*

Work, Helen Palmer describes the unhealthy Four's envy this way:

> Envy is the knife's twist in the heart when others enjoy the happiness that you long for. People seem to be content; they seem happy in their jobs and families. They seem to feel fulfilled, but you have been denied.[10]

The unhealthy Four will display their envy through jealousy. They can be envious of everything—relationships, possessions, health, hobbies, clothes, style…you name it. Nothing is off-limits. Unhealthy Fours perceive that everyone else has more of whatever it is they desire. They ask, "How are other people so happy? Why are other couples so attentive, so in tune with each other? What do they have that I am missing? Why can't *I* be happy for a change?"

What the Four can't seem to attain appears to be readily grasped by everyone else, so Fours feel like victims. To push back, unhealthy Fours act out their jealousy by being competitive. This can be especially hard for siblings to endure.

Unredeemed Fours put far too much emphasis on their feelings and mistakenly believe that they will find themselves somewhere within this compilation of emotions. They often get stuck mulling over their feelings to the point where they are drained to the dregs. To be in health, Fours must stop bathing in their feelings and mistaking them for their own identity or essence. They must stop playing with their moods and resist projecting them onto everyone else.

The path to waking up from this melancholy slumber is to receive the free gift of grace that Jesus offers, to be filled with the Holy Spirit, and then to allow God's Spirit to lead them into the truth of who they are. They are not a conglomerate of their emotions but rather a child of God and made in His likeness.

---

10. Palmer, *The Enneagram in Love and Work,* 109.

In relationships, the unhealthy Four has an idealistic image of their spouse that can never be realized. It becomes impossible for the Four to gloss over the imperfections because they live under the same roof, and their fantasy is shattered. When they finally get their perfect mate, it all turns into an empty shell of unrealistic expectations.

The turmoil in the relationship of an unhealthy Four can become impossible to endure. When they possess what they thought they wanted, the illusion bursts, the feelings come, and they find they don't really want it at all. There's a vicious back-and-forth struggle between the partners. When the Four's spouse moves toward greater transparency and vulnerability, the Four sees all of their imperfections and pulls back. When the partner then withdraws from the criticism and disapproval, the Four eases up and wants to share their deepest feelings and thoughts again.

HEALTHY FOURS

Fours find their *true self* and are most God-centered when they can balance their emotions, harness the power of their feelings, and live in the present. Healthy Fours experience equilibrium. They are thankful for the present and count their blessings rather than mull over all that has escaped them. They distance themselves from the drama of a melancholy outlook and focus on living in the real world, one that is rich in beauty, which they have a trained eye to observe.

WHEN THEY MOVE FROM FANTASY TO REALITY IN RELATIONSHIPS, HEALTHY FOURS ACCEPT THAT EVERY PERSON HAS THEIR OWN SET OF FLAWS.

When they move from fantasy to reality in relationships, healthy Fours realize that their friends and partners can never live up to their unrealistic expectations. They accept that every person has their own set of flaws. Fours must balance their expectations of others by reminding themselves that the deviations from perfection make an authentic original masterpiece. After all, Fours can really appreciate anything that's one-of-a-kind and not an imitation.

Healthy Fours recognize that we are all broken people, but God will put us back together again if we allow Jesus into our lives. They must keep in mind that our emotions can easily deceive us, and we must wrap ourselves up in Christ, not use our feelings as our security blanket. Jesus came to set us free from our fixations and bring us back to being centered on God. Healthy Fours finally find a depth of feeling and emotions that is only accessible to the redeemed.

BIBLICAL EXAMPLE: AMNON

I feel compelled to apologize for using such a troubled person as my biblical example, but Amnon is one of the clearest examples of an unhealthy Four found in Scripture. He serves as a warning to all Fours of the dangers of wallowing in their emotions and sadness.

Amnon was the oldest son of King David and his third wife, Ahinoam of Jezreel. Amnon had a half-brother named Absalom and a half-sister named Tamar, children of David and his fourth wife, Maacah. The Bible records his story this way:

> In the course of time, Amnon son of David fell in love with Tamar, the beautiful sister of Absalom son of David. Amnon became so obsessed with his sister Tamar that he made himself ill. She was a virgin, and it seemed impossible for him to do anything to her.   (2 Samuel 13:1–2)

It's important to note the distinction that Amnon "*made himself ill.*" He chose to fixate on someone who was not his to have.

He wore his feelings for Tamar like a garment marinating his skin until he was physically sick. He confused his desperate longing for her with his own identity and convinced himself that he would never be complete without her—an unhealthy obsession.

As we read further, Amnon's story demonstrates just why Fours need healthy people around them to guide them out of their melancholy moments, a support system to see clearly when emotions are clouding their judgment. As history shows, Amnon did not choose the right person and, unfortunately, received the worst possible advice.

> *Now Amnon had an adviser named Jonadab, son of Shimeah, David's brother. Jonadab was a very shrewd man. He asked Amnon, "Why do you, the king's son, look so haggard morning after morning? Won't you tell me?" Amnon said to him, "I'm in love with Tamar, my brother Absalom's sister." "Go to bed and pretend to be ill," Jonadab said. "When your father comes to see you, say to him, 'I would like my sister Tamar to come and give me something to eat. Let her prepare the food in my sight so I may watch her and then eat it from her hand.'"*
>
> (2 Samuel 13:3–5)

Other translations say Jonadab was "crafty" or "cunning." Guess who else is described in this manner? The snake that deceived Eve in the garden of Eden! (See Genesis 3:1.) Jonadab was a snake who did everything but fill in the blanks for Amnon. Like Eve, Amnon decided to partake of forbidden fruit and raped his sister. He acted upon his unredeemed longings and ruined lives as a result. That was some bad advice.

If Amnon's unspeakably horrific act was not bad enough, what he did next was unthinkable. It can only be understood through the framework of the type Four's makeup.

Then Amnon hated her with intense hatred. In fact, he hated her more than he had loved her. Amnon said to her, "Get up and get out!" "No!" she said to him. "Sending me away would be a greater wrong than what you have already done to me." But he refused to listen to her. He called his personal servant and said, "Get this woman out of my sight and bolt the door after her." So his servant put her out and bolted the door after her.   (2 Samuel 13:15–18)

When Amnon finally took what he longed for, it turned into a mirage. His feelings had lied to him, as feelings often do, and left him with nothing but unrealistic expectations. The passion his mind had convinced him was right ended with great shame and self-disgust. Learning nothing from his colossal crime, he spiraled even further downward by casting Tamar aside like an item that could be discarded. When led only by their emotions, Fours remain lost.

> A HEALTHY FOUR INTEGRATES TRAITS OF TYPE ONE, THE PERFECTIONIST, BECAUSE THEY NEED THE RULES AND BOUNDARIES THAT ONES SO CLEARLY SEE AND FOLLOW.

A Four moves toward health when they integrate to type One, the Perfectionist, because they need the rules and boundaries that Ones so clearly see and follow. If only Amnon's advisor had been a healthy One. Within boundaries and structure, a Four can begin to separate their feelings from facts and find their true identity.

The redeemed Four perceives and expresses the beauty of God's creation in original, inspired ways. Much of our world's finest art and poetry would be lost without Fours. They transform our broken existence into beauty, just as a timely word does in a crisis. Solomon wrote, *"A word fitly spoken is like apples of gold in settings of silver"* (Proverbs 25:11 NKJV). Fours bring us beauty out of the ashes.

Fours must stay within the parameters of God's commands and allow the Holy Spirit to bring them into balance. As *The Enneagram: A Journey of Self Discovery* notes, "Like Fours, Jesus was a 'man of sorrows', but he carefully avoided melancholy and self-pity. He did not portray himself as ultimately a tragic figure, but instead as on the way to becoming the triumphant Son of Man."[11]

A MEDIA PROFESSIONAL'S TESTIMONY

Here is the personal testimony of a young creative media professional who is a Four. He has learned to be healthy by calling out the beauty of others.

—

As the most misdiagnosed Enneagram personality, Fours often find themselves thrown into a crisis of self-discovery. Our fear is not having an identity or significance in life. My wife Audrey has many stories of me coming home after meeting a friend for the first time and stressing out about some offhand comment I made that I believe ruined that person's chances of realizing my importance. She can also tell you about other toxic times before I discovered the Enneagram.

I was and still am somewhat of an oversharer, as in, "I just met you five minutes ago, but here is my life story, including all the embarrassing details that 'normal people' hide behind the mask." This *flaw* is rooted in the fact that Fours just want to be understood; we want to be seen as unique and *the Individualist*. This longing translates to chasing a dream, achieving it, and then feeling empty because we have made that dream into so much more than it is.

---

11. Beesing, et al., *The Enneagram: A Journey of Self Discovery*, 70.

So, I have a message to all the Fours or possible Fours: get out of your head sometimes. You have a gift. You see the beauty in the world around you, with all of its flaws. Use it, and change those around you. They are hurting too; sometimes, they just need someone special to point out the beauty in their lives. The fulfillment this brings will help you discover that you *are* important. You might just be that form of special that you have sought so long to be.

8

TYPE FIVE – THE OBSERVER

Some Enneagram teachers have identified the barn owl as the animal that most represents type Five. They point out that you can be in a barn for many hours before suddenly looking up and realizing that this creature has been watching you the entire time. Like the barn owl, Fives are known as the Observer. Fives are always in their heads, always thinking and always observing.

In *The Enneagram: A Christian Perspective*, Richard Rohr and Andreas Ebert describe Fives as "discoverers of new ideas, researchers and inventors, objective, questioning, and interested in exploring things in detail. They can be original minds, provocative, surprising, unorthodox, and profound."[12]

This Enneagram type highly values privacy and will vigorously protect it. They are very careful to censor all private material from the eyes of the world. If a Five's confidence is betrayed and their

---

12. Rohr and Ebert, *The Enneagram: A Christian Perspective*, 115.

private life goes public, it is devastating to them. It is almost an ironclad guarantee that the perpetrator of the betrayal will never be given another chance to repeat the offense.

THE MOST WITHDRAWN OF ALL THE ENNEAGRAM TYPES, FIVES VIEW THE WORLD AS INVASIVE. THEY NEED THEIR PERSONAL TIME TO POWER BACK UP.

Fives require a designated retreat, a protected sanctum, a place where they can recharge and recenter their lives. For this reason, many Fives consider their homes to be their castle whose moats are mental constructs that say, "This far and no further." The most withdrawn of all the Enneagram types, Fives view the world as invasive. They need their personal time to power back up. Time alone and personal space are essential for Fives. In her overview of the nine Enneagram types, Beth McCord points out that the core weakness of a Five is "the feeling that you lack inner resources and that too much interaction with others will lead to catastrophic depletion."[13]

This Enneagram type's capital sin is avarice, but their greediness relates more to their mental and emotional resources. The Five's particular form of greed is shown when they withhold their energy and time for social interactions. If they are invited to an event and don't think it will be worth their while, they simply won't go. They are not hoarders of material things—in fact, Fives are the most minimalist of all the Enneagram types—but Fives will hoard whatever information ensures their freedom. They can also be greedy with the wealth of knowledge that they have accumulated.

Fives often compartmentalize their friends and relationships in an effort to manage their mental and emotional resources. They see relationships as liabilities that can drain their mental energies.

---

13. Beth McCord, *Enneagram Type 1: The Moral Perfectionist* (Nashville, TN: Thomas Nelson, 2019), 4.

They carefully identify which connections can be placed on *low-power mode*. Those in a friendship with a Five may find that they never know or meet any other friends of that Five. Subconsciously, a Five will often do this without any thought or effort.

All of this does not mean that Fives are not good friends. In fact, they are often surprised when others describe them as their "very best friend." Fives often have little to no need to verbally share these same sentiments. Though they would never advertise it, Fives are known for being gentle and caring, something you will never discover from a mere superficial relationship with them. They are often misunderstood as being detached, uncaring, and uninterested by those who do not know them well. This is not the persona they necessarily wish to display but often occurs because of their need to withdraw and recharge, along with their propensity to live inside of their heads.

In a work environment, Fives like to know their schedules and hate open-ended meetings; brainstorming sessions are highly distasteful to a Five. Their avarice with their coveted time causes them to view long meetings and unplanned events as invasions of their time and privacy. It is best to give Fives the freedom to prepare mentally for what will be required of them. For even better results, give them their own workspace. Misery for a Five is an open office where multiple conversations can be overheard, or worst yet, directed at them. With boundaries and a workspace, they are shielded from the intrusions of fellow workers sharing their feelings. They are sensitive to intrusions that most do not even identify as such. Allow a Five to work in solitude, where they are most comfortable. Don't ask them questions without limits or assign them ambiguous tasks. Give them clear expectations, define parameters for their work, set deadlines, and watch them perform at their highest level. Fives are overwhelmed easily with unexpected changes in direction or purpose. It is best to prepare them for these changes and give Fives time to process them. Too much, too fast, leads to a meltdown.

Paradoxically, Fives are great listeners because they will hear a matter completely through and can listen to others for hours at a time with no need to interrupt. This detachment makes them great counselors. They collect all the information before speaking. Thanks to their objectivity and ability to withdraw themselves emotionally from *drama*, they can hear the real issues, giving them the incredible ability to see more clearly and realistically than most. They will always think before they speak. Fives are known for their wisdom because they detach themselves from the person and really hear the matter dispassionately. Their words are always weighed and can be pure gold once spoken.

FIVES DO NOT CRITICIZE; THEIR NONJUDGMENTAL APPROACH TO LIFE PROVIDES THEM WITH A UNIQUE AND WONDERFUL SENSE OF HUMOR.

Fives do not criticize; their nonjudgmental approach to life provides them with a unique and wonderful sense of humor. Their sardonic wit enlivens any conversation. What makes Fives exceptionally funny is the exquisite comic timing of their humor that catches you so unexpectedly. Their broad knowledge provides endless material for their banter. If you're looking for a wise conversation that will keep you laughing, chat with a Five.

However, don't be in a rush. Pushing a Five for a quick opinion will be met with opposition. Allow them time to mull over a matter before you require an answer. Picking the brain of a Five is an arduous task. They will only share what they are willing to give in the context of their choosing, so it's best to ask specific questions within their clear area of expertise. Fives resist ambiguous open-ended questions that are spontaneous and not well prepared. Remember, you are on the clock with a Five—every minute counts with them—so ask them questions involving their interests.

Unlike other Enneagram types, when the possibility of entering into a relationship presents itself, Fives weigh out every aspect of it and count the potential cost. This is a hurdle in and of itself. They consider how much time the other person will require, and whether this person will be worth the pain and struggle that the Five will undoubtedly endure. Instinctively, Fives know it is easier for them to live alone, free to follow the pursuits of their own hearts. They have already considered that the other person will have needs and expectations; they know that there will be a certain loss of freedom, time, and energy. How different will the reality of the relationship be from their grandiose ideal? Fives carefully weigh it all out to determine if it is worth the effort. In *The Enneagram in Love and Work*, Helen Palmer says, "For Fives, love has less to do with romance than with deciding that a certain person is worth the price of pain."[14]

After the death of his best friend, Alfred Lord Tennyson wrote, "'Tis better to have loved and lost than never to have loved at all." These words can greatly encourage a Five to take a chance, count the cost, and embrace a relationship with another.

It is difficult for other types to understand the struggle of a Five because it takes place entirely inside their heads, and they're not prone to share their private thoughts. Many Fives do not want to appear to be hermits or aloof loners, yet their basic wiring can easily lead them there.

UNHEALTHY FIVES

The apostle Paul wrote, "*No one should seek their own good, but the good of others*" (1 Corinthians 10:24). When unhealthy Fives yield entirely to their greed, they are setting themselves up to be greatly misunderstood. From the outside looking in, stingy Fives appear to be disinterested and entirely detached, even from those

---

14. Palmer, *The Enneagram in Love and Work*, 133.

whom they love the most. This makes it difficult for their relationships to thrive.

Unhealthy Fives may find themselves alone and single in their old age. They often view children as inconvenient, needy, and time thieves. They may overthink their way out of meaningful relationships and withdraw when the time requirements to maintain such bonds are *imposed* upon them. The love life of a Five is especially daunting because it requires them to get out of their head and be led by their heart. Surrendering their mind to follow their heart goes against their very nature.

In the workspace, unhealthy Fives will show no initiative and remain silent when volunteers are sought. Their stinginess with their time can limit their opportunities for advancement, and they are not thought of as *team players*. This is a great tragedy because when their work is meaningful to them, nothing could be further from the truth. When they view their project as significant, they become determined and committed workers. Actually, finding a solution to a difficult problem motivates them more than the rewards that may follow. A challenging problem will bring out the best in them.

The basic fear of a Five is to be incapable, incompetent, or helpless. In disintegration, Fives move toward the manipulation techniques of type Seven, the Dreamer, which involve gluttony and excess. Unhealthy Fives will simply let themselves go when they can't solve a problem or overcome a hurdle; they turn to coping mechanisms when frustrated with their inability to find an answer. The real danger for a Five is their propensity to indulge in unhealthy and addictive habits to numb their pain. Drug or alcohol abuse, overeating, and other coping techniques are used to dull their keen Observer senses.

HEALTHY FIVES

To move toward health, Fives need to push themselves outward and force themselves to be generous with their time and resources. They need to open up their castle, let the drawbridge down, and invite people in. If this sounds like a lot of work that would require a herculean effort from you, then you are likely a Five, and this is just what the doctor ordered.

Proverbs 18:1 (ESV) says, *"Whoever isolates himself seeks his own desire; he breaks out against all sound judgment."* The simple truth is that no one was meant to do life alone; we *all* need other people in our lives. Healthy Fives reject their natural tendency to isolate themselves to seek their own desires. They show those they love their true feelings by being generous with their time. Fives are helped by friends who will encourage them to step out, give their time to others, and share all the knowledge they possess. A good friend will encourage a Five to try a new hobby, explore different activities, and even call them out when they are stingy with their time.

To be healthy, Fives must learn to let go and cut loose sometimes by silencing all the alarms going off in their brains to play it safe and hold back. Healthy Fives allow themselves the grace to make mistakes. They have learned that failures can be opportunities to fall forward.

> HEALTHY FIVES ARE HOSPITABLE, KIND, AND POLITE—DEEP WELLS OF COMPASSION, WISDOM, AND EMPATHY.

Fives move to health when they move toward type Eight, the Challenger, by asserting what they know to be true and becoming a force for good. Healthy Fives are hospitable, kind, and polite— deep wells of compassion, wisdom, and empathy. Their inner strength and genuine care are a source of comfort to those who are fortunate enough to be in their lives. Healthy Fives intentionally link their hearts to their wealth of knowledge and make room for others to participate in their lives. They are some of the warmest and funniest people to be around.

BIBLICAL EXAMPLE: MARY, THE MOTHER OF JESUS

Jesus's mother Mary demonstrated the traits of a Five in the biblical record we have of her responses to information she received. When the shepherds hurried to Bethlehem to see the baby Jesus and then spread the news that the angel announced the Messiah's birth, *"Mary treasured up all these things and pondered them in her heart"* (Luke 2:19).

When Jesus was twelve years old, the holy family went to Jerusalem for Passover with all of their relatives and friends. They didn't realize that Jesus had remained behind in the temple, so when they went back and found him, they reprimanded him.

> *"Why were you searching for me?" he asked. "Didn't you know I had to be in my Father's house?" But they did not understand what he was saying to them. Then he went down to Nazareth with them and was obedient to them. But his mother treasured all these things in her heart.*
>
> (Luke 2:49–51)

Mary was an observer and a thinker. Notice how she processed the angelic announcement that she would bear a son:

> *In the sixth month of Elizabeth's pregnancy, God sent the angel Gabriel to Nazareth, a village in Galilee, to a virgin named Mary. She was engaged to be married to a man named Joseph, a descendant of King David. Gabriel appeared to her and said, "Greetings, favored woman! The Lord is with you!" Confused and disturbed, Mary tried to think what the angel could mean.* (Luke 1:26–29 NLT)

Like a Five, Mary's initial reaction to this news was not from her gut or from her heart but from her head. She was thinking about what was said.

"Don't be afraid, Mary," the angel told her, "for you have found favor with God! You will conceive and give birth to a son, and you will name him Jesus. He will be very great and will be called the Son of the Most High. The Lord God will give him the throne of his ancestor David. And he will reign over Israel forever; his Kingdom will never end!" Mary asked the angel, "But how can this happen? I am a virgin." The angel replied, "The Holy Spirit will come upon you, and the power of the Most High will overshadow you. So the baby to be born will be holy, and he will be called the Son of God. What's more, your relative Elizabeth has become pregnant in her old age! People used to say she was barren, but she has conceived a son and is now in her sixth month." (Luke 1:30–36 NLT)

With this news, Mary, the Observer, rushed off to see Elizabeth for herself. *"A few days later Mary hurried to the hill country of Judea, to the town where Zechariah lived. She entered the house and greeted Elizabeth"* (Luke 1:39 NLT).

There, Elizabeth confirmed the news that Mary was carrying Jesus in her womb. Next, we discover how well young Mary processed the overwhelming information she was given.

Try to imagine how difficult this would have been for a young teenage girl, pregnant out of wedlock, in a culture that stoned girls for this crime. Mary was able to thoroughly think it all through and understand the tremendous implications of becoming the mother of Jesus. She responded:

"Oh, how my soul praises the Lord. How my spirit rejoices in God my Savior! For he took notice of his lowly servant girl, and from now on all generations will call me blessed. For the Mighty One is holy, and he has done great things for me."

(Luke 1:46–49 NLT)

And it was Mary who observed that the wine had run out at the wedding feast at Cana. She pointed this out to her Son, who performed His first public miracle, turning somewhere between 120 and 180 gallons of water into wine. (See John 2:1–11.)

A WORSHIP LEADER'S TESTIMONY

In chapter two, I shared the personal testimony of a twenty-eight-year-old worship leader who's a Five. His comments on the Enneagram are insightful in light of what we've just explored regarding the Observer:

> I really enjoy the Enneagram because it gives each of the nine types a lot to think about. Much of it can be really tough to hear, but it is incredibly freeing to feel so understood. The Enneagram gives me a lot to work on so I can continue my path of personal growth. It also has provided me with incredible empathy for all the other eight Enneagram types.

9

TYPE SIX – THE LOYALIST

Enneagram Sixes are recognized as the Loyalist because they are known for being dependable and dutiful in all of their relationships. You can count on them to be steadfast friends, family members, spouses, and parents. To be loved by a Six is to have a best friend for life.

The faithful friendships of Sixes are marked by their affection. When the Sixes greet someone they love, their salutations are genuine and intense. Their warm feelings are supported by their kind words. The apostle Peter demonstrated the Six's intensity when he greeted Jesus at breakfast in Galilee after the Lord's resurrection:

> *Early in the morning, Jesus stood on the shore, but the disciples did not realize that it was Jesus. He called out to them, "Friends, haven't you any fish?" "No," they answered. He said, "Throw your net on the right side of the boat and you will find some." When they did, they were unable to haul the net in*

because of the large number of fish. Then the disciple whom Jesus loved said to Peter, "It is the Lord!" As soon as Simon Peter heard him say, "It is the Lord," he wrapped his outer garment around him (for he had taken it off) and jumped into the water. The other disciples followed in the boat, towing the net full of fish, for they were not far from shore, about a hundred yards. When they landed, they saw a fire of burning coals there with fish on it, and some bread. (John 21:4–9)

Sixes show the most practical form of love. They will be quick to stay home with a sick loved one, take out the overflowing trash, or help a friend move. Sixes love you for who you are and not the image you portray. They can see the flaws, the cracks, and the negative traits and still stay one hundred percent committed. They are loyal to the individual, not to what they can provide or produce. They are low-maintenance partners who carry more than their fair share of responsibility. Sixes don't require a lot of attention, and their loyalty is without question to those to whom they are attached. They will put those people first and exemplify great sacrifice for the needs of others.

> SIXES SHOW THE MOST PRACTICAL FORM OF LOVE. THEY WILL BE QUICK TO STAY HOME WITH A SICK LOVED ONE, TAKE OUT THE OVERFLOWING TRASH, OR HELP A FRIEND MOVE.

To have the Six's allegiance is to have the most dependable and trustworthy friend, coworker, or family member. Their loyalty spills over into other areas such as work, sports, religion, and hobbies. To their detriment, when average to unhealthy, this allegiance can become the Six's Achilles' heel. They will often stand by others and their ideas long after it is time to let go.

Because they are workhorses, Sixes often mistakenly believe that they will be loved for all the work that they can accomplish, and they are often exploited for this reason. Their loyalty is driven by their deepest desire to have a sense of support, but it is often not rewarded. The huge amount of work they produce is not always from the goodness of their hearts, but instead from their great need for security. Loyalists invest a great deal into all of their relationships and convictions, unconsciously believing that their efforts will be honored with an increased sense of security and safety.

Sixes see and avoid potential problems before they arise. They have a sixth sense for danger. The outlook of a Six is that the world as a whole is a threatening place. Because of this, they are excellent troubleshooters. When unhealthy, this constant awareness of possible difficulties can leave the Six feeling anxious and overwhelmed, stuck in analysis paralysis. Their caution often leaves them suspicious of others, while their indecision keeps them uncertain of their own thoughts. Plagued with these doubts, the Six can become untrusting and defiant.

They will play the devil's advocate because they are sensitive to the weak spots in any position. Their doubts and insecurities will lead them to test an argument. At the same time, their cautionary approach often produces great powers of discernment. Sixes will go through all the possible scenarios looking for what could possibly go wrong. They lay all the cards on the table, face up. Perhaps this is why Sixes have great powers of imagination and are creative thinkers.

Sixes find great security in law and order, placing a high value on conforming to standards. They find their self-worth by carrying out delegated responsibilities and proving they are dependable. Sixes believe they are good when they are faithful, obedient, and loyal—in a word, responsible. Many Enneagram teachers believe that Sixes are the most common type in Western societies. The irony is that most people will not readily identify themselves as a Six.

Sixes often feel uncomfortable receiving praise, since their insecurities make them question its validity. They often silently wonder if the person giving the praise has ulterior motives, or plans to turn around and hurt them.

Faith—knowing that God is greater than all of their fears—can help Sixes alleviate their self-defeating tendencies. *"Faith is the substance of things hoped for, the evidence of things not seen"* (Hebrews 11:1 NKJV). Such faith is not based on seen threats or potential dangers, but rather on the evidence of the unseen God who is greater than every enemy.

Healthy Sixes learn to face their fears head-on, attack every problem with courage, and come to their own conclusions with certainty. A redeemed Six finds their true security in Jesus. They become a bedrock of stability for those who are in a relationship with them.

UNHEALTHY SIXES

An unhealthy Six allows their fear of abandonment to drive their decision-making. Alarmed by the uncertainties of life and all of the problems that come with it, they do not believe they are capable of taking on its challenges. As feelings of inferiority flair up, they often overcompensate and take on an air of superiority, trying to bluff their way forward.

While many different Enneagram types have a preoccupation with being attractive or in great shape, an unhealthy Six is motivated by the security they find when others approve of the way they look. Their fears disappear when others respect them for their physique or the way they present themselves.

The unhealthy Six's feelings of inferiority are often valid and self-fulfilling. They set themselves up for failure because their focus is too centered on survival. Using the analogy of a swimmer, they spend a great deal of energy treading water rather than pushing ahead toward a goal. This is where a good friend can encourage them in their endeavors and stick with them as they attempt to carry things through.

> UNHEALTHY SIXES NEED A GOOD FRIEND TO ENCOURAGE THEM IN THEIR ENDEAVORS AND STICK WITH THEM AS THEY ATTEMPT TO CARRY THINGS THROUGH.

An inward resistance to success accompanies an unhealthy Six's insecurity. Every new promotion brings situations full of unknown threats that can be scary. As the fear of change begins to set in, the memory of earlier victories vanishes from the unhealthy Six's mind. They are left feeling unprepared and underqualified for the task ahead. Paranoid, they begin to detach themselves from the facts and instead build a false *worst-case-scenario* reality. As their frightening illusion grows, they lose any remaining self-confidence and turn to codependency. They start to rely on people, beliefs, or structures to make decisions for them while simultaneously blaming their newfound support system for their problems.

Over time, these *safety nets* deteriorate and fall apart, causing an unhealthy Six to refuse to address the underlying problem: their own insecurities. When it all comes crashing down, their somewhat subdued panic, self-doubt, and suspicions come to the surface. The unhealthy Sixes then build a case against their own instincts and decision-making. It is a vicious cycle because as their anxiety grows, they find themselves grasping for yet another safety net. Left in this state, the Six disintegrates into an unhealthy Three. Attempting to save their own skin, they can become manipulative, dishonest, and unfaithful. Pathologically untrusting, the unhealthy Six shows signs of a deep-rooted hostility toward others and their environment. Ultimately, the unhealthy Six's first step to health is to name their anxiety for what it is: fear.

HEALTHY SIXES

When the Six comes to terms with their anxiety and chooses to let go of fear, they learn to trust their instincts and become the most balanced version of themselves. Able to foresee potential problems while still moving forward, the Six is liberated from the chains of anxiety and no longer stuck in analysis paralysis. The Six transforms into a gentle leader when self-confident and trusting of others. Healthy Sixes begin to make decisions without asking for permission, using previous victories to reassure themselves that they can minimize the risks. One of the greatest characteristics of the Six is that they can overcome fear faster than any other Enneagram type because they have learned to face so many of their own fears daily.

Sixes move to health when they move toward the calm and composure of the Enneagram Nine, the Peacemaker. The healthy Six has learned that laughter is the best medicine to drive out fear, and this facet of their personality comes through with their jokes and witty remarks. They find the balance between interdependence and independence, caution and courage, humility and leadership, reality and optimism, as well as disbelief and trust.

Dependable and sincere, no one will stand by you like a healthy Six. They are capable of enormous self-sacrifice for family, friends, and causes they believe in. They are endearing, easygoing team players who elicit warm emotions from others. Whether you meet them in childhood or college, the Loyalist is the kind of friend you will have for life.

The Six's ultimate conversion from fear to courage can only take place when they truly encounter Jesus. It is then that they grasp Jesus's steadfastness and know deep within their soul that He is their ultimate safety net. The unconditional love they find in Christ is stronger than fear. *"There is no fear in love. But perfect love drives out fear*" (1 John 4:18). Jesus is a never-ending source of security and, in Him, the Six can finally find peace.

BIBLICAL EXAMPLE: PETER

Many identify Peter as a type Six. In true Loyalist fashion, Peter was very vocal about his allegiance to Jesus, genuinely believing and wholeheartedly claiming that he would never deny his Lord. In the face of danger, Peter demonstrated the two prominent characteristics of a Six: courage and cowardice. In a single night, Peter cut off a guard's ear in an attempt to protect Jesus... and then denied Christ not once but three times. (See John 18:10; 18:17–27.)

Peter's latter actions do not point to a lack of sincerity in his repeated claims throughout the Gospels to loyally stand by Jesus. Everything inside of him wanted to remain faithful, but the fear for his safety won the battle. This denial demonstrates the inner turmoil that is constantly churning inside a Six. They experience a continuous battle between steadfastness and self-preservation.

Peter was truly heartbroken and humiliated after denying Christ. (See Matthew 26:75; Luke 22:62.) He faced the deep shame of knowing that he had abandoned Jesus. But he himself was not forsaken or abandoned by Jesus for his failure—and neither are we! The breakfast in Galilee by the sea after Jesus's resurrection is one of the most touching accounts of grace in the entire Bible. As recounted in John 21, the risen Lord restores and reassures Peter of their relationship while cooking breakfast for His disciples.

Peter's setback gave him the courage to face future dangers head-on and ultimately die a martyr for His Jesus. A Christ-centered Six possesses the potential to exercise amazing fortitude.

A 29-YEAR-OLD SIX'S TESTIMONY

Here is the personal testimony of a man, age twenty-nine, who discovered the power of the Enneagram enlightened by grace.

—

As far back as I can remember, I just thought that everybody thought and processed things the same way. After learning about the Enneagram and studying the different types, I understood that people are wired quite differently. This has given me a newfound grace for my personal relationships and for people in general.

When it comes to the Six specifically, it made me feel really understood. It allowed me to extend grace to myself by clearly exposing my strengths and weaknesses. The thing that stood out the most is understanding that the fear aspect of a Six isn't always negative but can also be a positive tool to foresee potential troubles.

When I became a committed follower of Jesus, I had to separate from many of my old friends. Because I am a Loyalist, this was so painful for me, but it had to be done. Now I understand why it was so difficult, and I also realize that even with the knowledge of how I am wired as a Six, I know I can only become the best version of myself with the help of the Holy Spirit.

One of my favorite discoveries was learning the different levels of health listed by the Enneagram Institute. (Visit www.enneagraminstitute.com for more information.) In my efforts to become a healthier Six, these levels provide a practical application and goals I can work toward.

10

TYPE SEVEN – THE ENTHUSIAST

Enneagram Sevens are known as the Enthusiast because of their humor, love of life, and playful antics. Sevens can often be overheard saying things like, "Let's go somewhere and just have fun!" Sevens are curious, always looking for the next entertaining adventure. They fill their calendars with new, fun, and exciting events and pull others into their escapades.

Sevens view life as a smorgasbord of experiences, which can range from tanning on a beach to bungee jumping. They are spontaneous and quick to act on any opportunity for merriment. In fact, their creed is *the more, the merrier*, in both participants and indulgence. The threat of being stuck with no opportunities for fun can instill a sense of panic.

Because Sevens are dreamers, they find great pleasure in the mental exercise of anticipating scheduled events. Their basic need *to be satisfied* drives them onward.

Sevens are the most optimistic of all the Enneagram types. They love to live in the future, relishing experiences not yet enjoyed. While there may be a great disparity between the ideal relationship, event, or vacation and the actual experience, this is no barrier for Sevens, who can immediately move on to the next great adventure in their minds. Their optimism soars, and they become overly enthusiastic. Sevens are helped by others who force them to face present realities and by those who encourage them to first count the cost before they leap.

> SEVENS CAN SHAKE OFF FAILURE IN A SPECTACULAR FASHION AS THEY ARE MENTALLY WELL TRAINED TO LIVE IN THE FUTURE RATHER THAN THE PAIN OF THE PAST.

Sevens can shake off failure in a spectacular fashion as they are mentally well trained to live in the future rather than the pain of the past. Setbacks that could take other people years to overcome are a mere speed bump for a Seven. They spend their days spinning every failure into a silver lining or a hidden blessing. This works for them until the loss is so great that painting it as a success is no longer possible. This scenario is devastating for them. The emotional swings of a Seven can be dramatic.

Their basic fear is to be trapped in pain, without any alternatives or way out. Because they are such fun-loving persons, Sevens have a real problem with the darker side of life. As children, many Sevens were literally afraid of the dark and needed night lights. Sevens like primary and bright colors when given an option.

Sevens will not linger long with their negative emotions, making it almost impossible for them to dwell on their pain. When suffering confronts them, they escape quickly to the more positive possibilities that can be found in the future. The rush of new and exciting events, activities, and people is the Seven's defense mechanism to distance them from the dark side of life with all its suffering and negativity. It really doesn't matter if all those new projections actually ever take place; their relief is found simply in the mental exercise of imagining the next fun adventure.

Sevens live in their heads, which comes as a shock to many because they seem to be so heart-centered. Their outward charm, engaging smiles, and overall brightness is misleading. Sevens hope they can please others by planning enjoyable activities, not having heart-to-heart talks.

Naturally leery of authoritarian figures, Sevens are very often self-employed. Bosses are seen as restraints who can limit or rein in the Seven's wild and free spirit. Their philosophy is, "Why live in a corral when you can run in the open plains?" Sevens prefer their freedom; they don't like to be boxed in. They frequently are found working several interesting jobs at the same time. A Seven works to keep as many options on the table as possible. This ensures the optimal amount of escape routes.

On the flip side of this, the potential discomfort that accompanies conflict also keeps Sevens from accepting supervisory positions. This enables them to dodge any unpleasant feelings that may come with the expectation of controlling their subordinates. Self-employment fits well with their desire to avoid pain at all costs.

Sevens can provide others with a much-needed reprieve from the monotony and drudgery of life. They gravitate toward the sunny side of life and provide a brighter outlook to those around them. Their natural cheerfulness is contagious. More serious Enneagram types may complain that any Sevens they know "never grew up."

The Seven's playfulness can generally lighten up a room, but an immature Seven can have quite the opposite effect in difficult situations. Their refusal to open themselves up to pain leaves them ill-equipped to know the appropriate responses to it. Their excessive need for fun, joy, and pleasure frequently causes them to try to cheer up others with comic relief or upbeat comments at the most inappropriate times. Their remarks at the death of a loved one are often too positive, or too fast, making them appear insensitive. This is not their intent; it is simply their defense mechanism against pain kicking in. When Sevens witness someone being physically hurt in an accident, their initial reaction is frequently nervous laughter. This, too, can bring them the scorn of those around them.

THE "LIFE IS MEANT TO BE FUN" ATTITUDE OF THE SEVEN CAN BRING MISUNDERSTANDINGS. THEY ARE OFTEN ON TO THE NEXT NEW THING BEFORE THE LAST ONE IS COMPLETE.

The *life is meant to be fun* attitude of the Seven can bring with it other misunderstandings. Sevens are often seen as those who never finish a project or venture. They are often on to the next new thing before the last one is complete. Whether unconsciously or intentionally, this may be because they are avoiding closure. For a Seven, completing an assignment or reaching a goal means having one less option. Open-ended projects are far more attractive to Sevens, who are actually very hard workers for causes they care about.

UNHEALTHY SEVENS

Though they themselves are frequently not aware of their own inner motivation, the need to avoid pain causes the Seven to fixate on always planning the next thing. A Seven who has not found balance and health will live for tomorrow rather than the present. What they have today is never enough, so they exist in a constant underlying state of discontentment. They must allow the Holy Spirit to teach them, as He did the apostle Paul, *"to be content whatever the circumstances"* (Philippians 4:11).

For the unrestrained Seven, *more is always better.* Their root sin is intemperance or gluttony. Without restraint, this can lead to weight problems; you will often find a Seven on some kind of a diet, even though they detest diets because of their basic fear of pain and deprivation. As pleasure-seekers, Sevens love food and desserts.

Like Twos, the Helper, and Nines, the Peacemaker, Sevens are especially prone to addiction. Unhealthy Sevens talk too much, indulge too much, and play too much. They may use drugs or alcohol to deaden the pain and artificially inflate their need for happiness.

When they bring others into their indulgences, the intemperance of a Seven often harms those people, but it frequently causes even greater damage to the Seven themselves. They can easily play the clown role because they have performed it on many occasions. But looking beyond the façade, the laughter and the smiles, you can unravel their deception. While they are busy being the life of the party, they are also running from the deep sadness they fear. They long for someone to take them seriously, to understand it's all a charade, but this is a formidable task because they have to convince others that they are always on top. The persona they project is actually a deterrent that keeps others from understanding the depth of who they really are.

The movie *Amadeus*[15] depicts Wolfgang Amadeus Mozart as an unhealthy Seven in an unforgettable exposé. Even Mozart's closest companions could not comprehend the depth of his pain. With no one to understand him, he continually relapsed into his well-rehearsed clown role and suffered from the way other people amused themselves at his expense. This movie accentuates the need for real accountability and support from the right people in our lives, Sevens included. It highlights our need for a Savior from ourselves and the ruin we can all face when left to our own devices.

---

15. *Amadeus*, directed by Miloš Forman (1984; Orion Pictures).

HEALTHY SEVENS

Sevens grow by learning to deal with their pain, staying and facing it rather than avoiding or fleeing from it. To become healthy, Sevens must travel the dark journey of engaging their pain, contemplating it, and then digesting it. This process is a difficult journey but so necessary for their well-being.

Sevens move to health when they migrate toward the mental soundness and stability of the Five, the Investigator. It is healthy for them to become more observant like Fives and slow down long enough to remain in the moment rather than constantly living in the future. The endless planning, the chatter, the distractions, and addictions must cease, and they must reconcile that all of this present life is not happy and beautiful. It is in this silence and stillness that Sevens become whole. This repose forces them to quit pretending that *all of life is nice.*

HEALTHY SEVENS HAVE LEARNED THAT NOT ALL LIMITATIONS IN LIFE ARE BAD; SOME ACTUALLY KEEP US FROM DANGER.

Healthy Sevens have learned that not all limitations in life are bad; some actually keep us from danger. The brakes on a bicycle are most welcome when going down a steep mountain trail, the highway railings around a steep curve keep us from falling off a cliff, and the perimeters of the Word of God protect us from eternal loss.

The gift or fruit of the Spirit that Sevens can inject into our world is joy. Healthy Sevens enjoy happy experiences, but they also know the contentment that joy alone can bring. Healthy Sevens know that true joy does not originate from living for our own selfish desires. God's Word instructs us to abandon a life of self-gratification for a life of serving others.

*Let nothing be done through selfish ambition or conceit, but
in lowliness of mind let each esteem others better than himself. Let each of you look out not only for his own interests,
but also for the interests of others. Let this mind be in you
which was also in Christ Jesus, who, being in the form of
God, did not consider it robbery to be equal with God, but
made Himself of no reputation, taking the form of a bond-
servant, and coming in the likeness of men. And being found
in appearance as a man, He humbled Himself and became
obedient to the point of death, even the death of the cross.*

(Philippians 2:3–8 NKJV)

Jesus declared, "Whoever loses his life for my sake and the gospel's will save it" (Mark 8:35 ESV). Cultural messages tell us otherwise, but stop and think about the folks you know who are totally
self-focused. Would you describe them as joyful? Do they appear
to be authentically happy? And what about you? In what areas of
your life are you most prone to adopt a self-serving attitude? Are
you generally the happiest in those areas?

When Sevens cooperate with God and embrace all facets
of life—the good, the bad, and the ugly—they pass through the
tomb of death into resurrection's morning. They bring our world
joy and hope like no other type. The joy they bring is not superficial or simply conjured up by human efforts, but is a sober joy that
is authentic, deep, and real.

Healthy Sevens generously give their gift of joy to those who
require it the most. They grow by putting themselves in the shoes
of others who need their empathy along with their good nature.
They no longer need to look away from those who are suffering,
for they have matured to a place of grace that allows them to pour
their gift of authentic cheer upon those with greatest need of it.
Only mature Sevens who have learned that God accepts them in
their entirety, not just their fun and sunny side, can emit this kind

of joy. In a world entirely too dark and hopeless, these healthy Sevens are desperately needed.

BIBLICAL EXAMPLE: KING SOLOMON

King Solomon was the son of David and the third king of Israel. Like his father, Solomon reigned for forty years, probably from around 970 to 931 BC. He is the quintessential example of an unhealthy Seven left with no restraints or limitations.

> *King Solomon was greater in riches and wisdom than all the other kings of the earth. All the kings of the earth sought audience with Solomon to hear the wisdom God had put in his heart.* (2 Chronicles 9:22–23)

While Solomon is revered even today for his wisdom, he's also renowned for his sin. He married foreign women and indulged in idolatry.

> *King Solomon loved many foreign women…Solomon clung to these in love. He had 700 wives, who were princesses, and 300 concubines. And his wives turned away his heart. For when Solomon was old his wives turned away his heart after other gods, and his heart was not wholly true to the* LORD *his God, as was the heart of David his father.* (1 Kings 11:1–4 ESV)

Where did all of his indulgences lead Solomon? Did he find happiness or, more specifically, joy in all his adventures? Our answer is found in the book of Ecclesiastes, an extended discourse on life's meaning that is traditionally considered to be authored by Solomon. It clearly describes the emptiness Sevens find at the end of unlimited indulgences. It begins:

> *The words of the Preacher, the son of David, king in Jerusalem. Vanity of vanities, says the Preacher, vanity of vanities! All is vanity.* (Ecclesiastes 1:1–2 ESV)

This book opens and ends with the same conclusion. (See Ecclesiastes 12:8.) It shows what it looks like to spend life in the mere pursuit of pleasure. Solomon writes:

> *I have seen all the things that are done under the sun; all of them are meaningless, a chasing after the wind.*
>
> (Ecclesiastes 1:14)

Solomon concludes that everything in life is meaningless when pleasure is the ultimate goal. Without God, all of our efforts are pointless. Sevens left to themselves remain on the gerbil wheel of endless pursuits and, in the end, are left wanting. In his final words, King Solomon urges us to obey God rather than seeking this path:

> *Now all has been heard; here is the conclusion of the matter: fear God and keep his commandments, for this is the duty of all mankind. For God will bring every deed into judgment, including every hidden thing, whether it is good or evil.*
>
> (Ecclesiastes 12:13–14)

Healthy Sevens give away their gift for seeking joy rather than spending it on themselves.

11

TYPE EIGHT – THE CHALLENGER

Let me start off by saying that if you are an Eight reading this chapter, bravo! You have already demonstrated more health than most people of your Enneagram type. Eights do not want to feel vulnerable or exposed; most view transparency as a threat. Vulnerability is perceived as flinching or turning their back to potential enemies who may want to take advantage of them.

Most Eights are quick to dismiss all personality tests and profiles by saying something like, "I'm not into all of that." Although they reject these tools, perhaps no other type needs the personal insights more than an Eight. On a side note, if you do not challenge your test result, you are probably not an Eight.

Eights are the greatest driving force of all the Enneagram types. Direct and assertive, they need control over their possessions and people. The all-important question for the Eight is,

"Who has power, and how do I assume it?" And then the question becomes, "How do I keep it now that I have it?"

Eights immediately survey the room to see who is in charge; soon afterward, they mentally assemble a pecking order of those present. They want to size up and know their competition. They want to know who is worthy of their esteem or deserving of their disdain. They turn everything into a fight or a sparring match. They will use intimidation, conflict, or any means possible to flush out the strong from the weak.

Eights will temporarily take the opposing view in a conversation, even if they don't believe it, just to start a skirmish. If they make an error in the middle of a debate, you will seldom see them back down. Being obsessed with power, they will turn an argument in any direction necessary to ultimately come out the victor. This is their way of sizing up the room and determining who is worthy of their trust and time. Eights are known for stirring up the pot and enjoying the process.

Passion for life, power, and the upper hand push an Eight to their limits. They work until they drop, play with all the gusto they can muster, and will be the last person out of the room when it's time to celebrate. They possess a lust for intensity.

> PASSION FOR LIFE, POWER, AND THE UPPER HAND PUSH AN EIGHT TO THEIR LIMITS. THEY WORK UNTIL THEY DROP AND PLAY WITH ALL THE GUSTO THEY CAN MUSTER.

Others can earn an Eight's respect by holding their own. Eights test everyone to determine if they are worthy of a relationship. It is a mistake to back down or soften your opinion for an Eight. Toe-to-toe confrontations earn their esteem. It is okay if you don't agree with them; just be sure you have an unwavering opinion. You will rarely change their minds, but you will earn their respect for standing firm.

Eights are natural leaders. People line up quickly behind an Eight when something needs to be done, most especially when it is a matter of justice or fairness. Eights will fight for the cause of the defenseless, the oppressed, and the marginalized because of their passion for justice and truth.

In *The Enneagram: A Christian Perspective*, Richard Rohr and Andreas Ebert describe Eights this way:

> Behind a façade of hardness, invulnerability, curses, or even brutality – there is a little boy or a little girl. This inner child is the exact opposite of the strength and power they outwardly project.[16]

The tenderness and vulnerability Eights possess are buried deep within them and only revealed to a few trusted people in their lives.

Eights will let down their guard with children and show their real warmth. The innocence of a child is no threat to an Eight, so they display a side of themselves to little ones that most adults will never see. Occasionally, the little child within an Eight that brings them such insecurity will discover this innocent vulnerability in others. When this occurs, an Eight will often rally to protect them.

Eights scarcely give praise, but no one is harder on an Eight than themselves. For this reason, they can be extremely hard on others. Eights will vigorously defend those they love, yet at the same time, these people may never know how much they are loved and respected.

The prominent need of an Eight is *to be against*. They can readily identify with Jesus when He said, "*Whoever is not with me is against me*" (Matthew 12:30).

The irony of an Eight is that their main concern is personal freedom. They want no one to control them, and yet they

16. Rohr and Ebert, *The Enneagram: A Christian Perspective*, 163–164.

attempt—and usually succeed—to control anything or anyone that has piqued their interest. To ensure that no one dominates them, they dominate others.

Eights find it difficult to delegate and will only do so to those who have earned their highest trust. Even in these cases, they will demand a detailed report on every aspect of the endeavor. As mentioned in chapter six on the Achiever, Eights and Threes are often misidentified for one another because in many situations, both types operate in a very similar manner. I have found that one of the best ways to determine between the types is found in their regard for the details. When given a report, a Three will go directly to the bottom line and then only ask details that they deem important; on the other hand, an Eight will absorb all of the line items on the report, demanding exact details, and also give the same great attention to the bottom line that the Three will display. This report test usually reveals whether someone is a Three or an Eight.

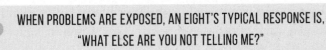

WHEN PROBLEMS ARE EXPOSED, AN EIGHT'S TYPICAL RESPONSE IS, "WHAT ELSE ARE YOU NOT TELLING ME?"

When problems are exposed, an Eight's typical response is, "What else are you not telling me?" Ambiguity is eyed suspiciously as a red flag or hidden agenda. Even an innocent oversight can mushroom into a nuclear meltdown for an Eight. They are always on the lookout for betrayal, so they hate to be blindsided by poor information and become immediately suspicious when it occurs. They may respond with a barrage of questions: "What else am I unaware of? Who is responsible? Why wasn't I informed?" Their suspicion can quickly turn into contempt for the poor soul whom they identify as the guilty party. In such cases, the best defense for that person is absolute transparency.

The basic fear of an Eight is being harmed, controlled, and violated. This leads them into their basic desire to protect themselves.

It is not uncommon for Eights to have personal bunkers, the best home security systems, and nightly checks to make sure the windows and doors are locked. They will survey any room they enter for possible threats. Those around an Eight may view them as paranoid. If this is voiced, the Eight will soundly reject this opinion as naivety, removing any possibility that they may be seen as weak. An Eight believes that only the strong survive, and they have no intention of losing their advantage.

An Eight may talk about a project or venture in such a way that others believe they are highly invested in it, but often, the Eight was just thinking out loud. The friend of an Eight leader once told me, "I never get too concerned about the next new adventure until they start writing big checks."

UNHEALTHY EIGHTS

Eights hate bullies, but an unhealthy Eight will be the biggest bully of them all. An unhealthy Eight will fixate on revenge, and all those who are viewed as disloyal to them will feel the Eight's full fury. Anger is their emotion of choice.

Eights move to disintegration when they pick up the unhealthy habits of a Five, the Observer, such as remaining silent and withdrawing from those around them. Unhealthy Eights will also utilize strategic giving to have things their way. They attach strings of control to their generosity and very often expect something of equal value in return. Unhealthy Eights will even manipulate their own partners' affection in this manner.

They will impose rigid rules on others yet will bend them to their own personal advantage. They will shamelessly demand that others toe the line while making extraordinary exceptions for themselves. Often, they act without considering how it affects others because it's *their way or the highway*. Because they are so self-absorbed, they never take into consideration the perspective of others. Unhealthy Eights justify their actions by reasoning that people should take care of their own interests. They reason that everyone else looks out for number one, so they should too. Eights are gut-based people who feel and act for their own interests.

The person most likely to deceive the Eight is the person who stares back at them in the mirror. They keep their defenses high with everyone else but relax them with themselves. Their ability to *smell a rat* is keen…except when it comes to discerning their own motives.

Those who wish to help an unhealthy Eight must question them in a straightforward manner because they seldom examine their motives. They are so fixated on their goals and accomplishing them that they can be clueless about their own selfish desires. The amount of self-centeredness they exhibit can be obvious to everyone around them, without even a hint of it dawning on them. This occurs because people's reactions to their decisions are inconsequential to Eights. They are inclined to believe that their own opinion is absolutely correct, so why question it? The Eight thinks, "If people don't like it, that's their problem."

HEALTHY EIGHTS

The virtue of an Eight is innocence. A redeemed Eight allows the Holy Spirit to guide them into protective roles for the most vulnerable. They become a force of good and capable of moving mountains. When outwardly focused, they leverage their need *to be against* by taking on the world's injustices and poverty. This world would look far worse without them; we desperately need Eights to lead the fight against wrongdoing and deceit. Their determination and grit have championed many causes that bring good to our world. Their ability to allow the criticism of others to roll off their backs while holding their ground has won many an important battle.

> **YOU CAN FIND HEALTHY EIGHTS MENTORING A COWORKER WHO THEY FEEL HAS BEEN OVERLOOKED OR TAKING THE NEXT PROSPECT UNDER THEIR WINGS.**

You can find healthy Eights mentoring a coworker who they feel has been overlooked or taking the next prospect under their wings. They know how to succeed and, in turn, fight for the success of others. For all of their Challenger strength, however, Eights must acknowledge their weaknesses and humble themselves under the mighty hand of God. They, too, need to ask for His forgiveness and yield entirely to the Potter's hand. Those Eights who do so are truly powerhouses because they have discovered the real source of strength.

Healthy Eights reconcile the innocent child inside of them with the reality that total control of one's own life is merely a mirage. As Helen Keller noted:

> Security is mostly a superstition. It does not exist in nature, nor do the children of men as a whole experience it. God Himself is not secure, having given man dominion over His works! Avoiding danger is no safer in the long run than outright exposure. The fearful are caught as often as the bold. Faith alone defends. Life is either a daring adventure or nothing. To keep our faces toward change and behave like free spirits in the presence of fate is strength undefeatable.[17]

We are all one heartbeat away from eternity. Tomorrow is not promised, nor is our safety from the calamities that life can bring. Despite all of our best efforts, life cannot be controlled but must be surrendered into the hands of Jesus. Healthy Eights relax their grip on life, on those around them, and, most importantly,

---

17. Helen Keller, *Let Us Have Faith* (New York: Doubleday, Doran & Co., 1940), 50–51.

on themselves. They lean into their heavenly Father's embrace and become like a child. They allow their softer side to be developed, becoming vulnerable and humble before the God of the universe, without denying the strengths that He has given them.

I think it's worth repeating that Eights and Threes can make a marvelous team if Eights can give up their need for control and allow Threes to have some measure of autonomy. Eights who are too immature or unhealthy to allow for this will, in short order, drive the Three away. This is a real loss because these two types have great synergy when they work together.

The invitation to the Eight is mercy. By integrating toward the Two's role of helping others, Eights begin to peak. These Eights hold out mercy to a world that is broken and offer it to their own brokenness in turn. When we clearly see our own imperfections, we find more grace to extend it to others. Redeemed and truly surrendered to the causes of Christ, Eights turn into champions of heroic proportions. They are softened in their hearts while still strong in leadership and demeanor.

BIBLICAL EXAMPLE: LABAN

Laban first appears in the Bible in Genesis 24:29–60. In his debut, he is shown to be in control of his father's household. Laban, not his father, was the decisive one who made things happen when Abraham's servant came to find a wife for Isaac. As Eights often do, when Laban received all of the information from Abraham's servant, he made a command decision and jumped all in. Laban leaped at the opportunity to acquire more wealth and power.

It is also interesting to note that when Rebekah was asked whether she wanted to stay home or leave with the servant (verse 58), she showed no hesitation to leave—perhaps to get out from under Laban's control. Rebekah's choice to leave is the same choice his own daughters made, without hesitation, decades later.

Born twenty years after Isaac and Rebekah's marriage, Jacob began to work for his uncle Laban as an adult. Though Jacob was an unhealthy Three at the time, he met his match in Laban, who used strategic giving to control Jacob's life. Laban promised his youngest daughter Rachel to Jacob as his bride in return for seven years of service. Laban then tricked Jacob into marrying his oldest daughter Leah instead. Jacob then had to serve Laban for seven more years to wed Rachel.

Laban demonstrates three typical Eight actions in his trickery:

1. His motivation for his deception was to protect the vulnerable—he didn't want his oldest daughter Leah to become an old maid.

2. He bent his own rules to his own advantage.

3. He extended his control over Jacob's life with strategic giving by promising Jacob his daughter Rachel if he would serve him an additional seven years.

Jacob knew that the unhealthy Eight he worked for would never agree to give him what was rightfully his. He was forced to flee without telling Laban of his departure. His conversation with his wives about that decision is most telling:

> "You know how hard I have worked for your father, but he has cheated me, changing my wages ten times. But God has not allowed him to do me any harm"...Rachel and Leah responded, "That's fine with us! We won't inherit any of our father's wealth anyway. He has reduced our rights to those of foreign women. And after he sold us, he wasted the money you paid him for us."   (Genesis 31:6–7, 14–15 NLT)

In the end, Jacob reached the conclusion that the only way to win with Laban was to get out from under his control. Jacob described what this control looked like in the following angry outburst at his uncle/father-in-law:

I worked for you through the scorching heat of the day and through cold and sleepless nights. Yes, for twenty years I slaved in your house! I worked for fourteen years earning your two daughters, and then six more years for your flock. And you changed my wages ten times! In fact, if the God of my father had not been on my side—the God of Abraham and the fearsome God of Isaac—you would have sent me away empty-handed. But God has seen your abuse and my hard work. That is why he appeared to you last night and rebuked you! (Genesis 31:40–42 NLT)

Laban, the boss, saw Jacob's flight as betrayal, which is precisely how Eights respond when critical information is withheld from them.

"What do you mean by deceiving me like this?" Laban demanded. "How dare you drag my daughters away like prisoners of war? Why did you slip away secretly? Why did you deceive me? And why didn't you say you wanted to leave?" (Genesis 31:26–27 NLT)

Vengeance was Laban's immediate fixation, anger was his emotion of choice, and all of this was fed by the threat of losing some of his power and wealth. Only God's intervention could keep Laban from causing Jacob harm. While Laban was pursuing Jacob, God appeared to him in a dream and warned him to leave Jacob alone. (See verse 29). Even with this divine encounter, however, Laban still insists that everything Jacob has taken rightfully belongs to him! (See verse 43.) And yet Jacob's angry confrontation, combined with the warning from God, apparently softens Laban a little—so long as Jacob promises to never mistreat Laban's daughters. They make a pact and set up a monument to seal the deal. Laban declares God *"is a witness to this covenant between us"* (Genesis 31:50 NLT) and the two men must never harm each other (verse 52).

The last we see of Laban, he has finally softened and is a better man because of it. *"Laban got up early the next morning, and he kissed his grandchildren and his daughters and blessed them. Then he left and returned home"* (Genesis 31:55 NLT).

Laban stands as a marvelous example of the incredible transformation and balance God can bring into an Eight's life. His strength is used to ensure the security of his daughters and their children, and his tenderness is openly displayed with his warmth toward them at his departure. Laban's strength was reined in by a holy God. This is the complete picture of a redeemed Eight.

12

TYPE NINE – THE PEACEMAKER

Positioned at the top of the Enneagram diagram, Nines are known as the Peacemaker. Above all else, they want to eliminate conflict and bring harmony into every situation. They can discern when someone or something is not in sync and immediately set out to bring all parties together. You will often hear them asking, "Why can't we all just get along?" Nothing is more important to a Nine than peace and reconciliation.

Nines prefer group activities where they can go with the flow. This removes the pressure of having to choose a side, which could cause potential conflict. It is much easier for them to allow others to make the decisions since the Nines find it difficult to be in touch with what they want. The mental exercise of personal decisions can be exhausting, isolating, and threatening for a Nine. They are not comfortable choosing for themselves and will often ask others, "What do *you* think?" Acting independently can make them feel isolated and alone. Because it is easier for Nines to know what they *don't* want than what they do, you can help them decide by leading them through the process of elimination. A defining characteristic of this type is that they will obsessively wrestle with personal decisions.

Nines are excellent mediators because they are capable of seeing so many different points of view. They see all sides to the question without personal bias. This perspective makes it genuinely difficult for them to make decisions. While those on either side of Nine—One, the Reformer, and Eight, the Challenger—are the most candid of the Enneagram types, Nines remain indirect and capable of putting everyone at ease. Ones and especially Eights often intimidate others with their straightforward approach, but the secret to the Nine's efficiency is their gentleness. They are disarming and inspire trust. Conflict is frightening to them, and as a result, their diplomacy presents a safe place for others to voice their opinions.

NINES' INTENSE FOCUS ON THEIR EMOTIONAL SURROUNDINGS OFTEN LEAVES THEM WITHOUT A PERSONAL OPINION AND OUT OF TOUCH WITH THEIR OWN FEELINGS.

The basic desire to make peace at all costs can cause Nines to lose themselves in the process. Their intense focus on their emotional surroundings has Nines finding themselves without a personal opinion and out of touch with their own feelings. The root sin of a Nine is sloth, demonstrated in the lethargic and self-forgetting way they approach their individuality. Because of their profound ability to understand others, it is difficult for a Nine to take a stand or view. They do not recognize their own, apart from their peers. This is especially difficult for them if it means opposing those close to them. A Nine is helped by being challenged to stand up for what they believe and thereby making a difference in the world.

Nines opt out of the drama and can go through life as mere spectators. Their deep desire to take the path of least resistance keeps them from developing as their own person. They are notorious for losing themselves in the people around them, living their lives vicariously through others, and avoiding conflict in the process. This approach to life denies them proper self-care and attention. The apathy they practice toward their own needs and desires keeps them on the sidelines of life because it's just easier for them to remain observers. If their external world is okay and at peace, then they believe they are okay as well. As noted in *The Enneagram: A Journey of Self Discovery*, Nines "often lack a natural and spontaneous reaction to what is happening, and that is one of the main problems which they typically fail to recognize."[18]

Many Nines feel, or have felt, overlooked because they are predisposed to just go along with others. They follow the program to maintain the comfort of neutrality and conserve personal energy. Their own needs seem to complicate things and require them to expend energy that they don't want to give. Others may see the Nine's self-nurturing and self-protection as a desire to remain independent, but nothing is further from the truth. Their greatest fear is loss, separation, and fragmentation.

Nines often feel inadequate to tackle the challenges their personal life presents. They are not equipped with the specific tools or emotions to successfully dissect their personality. Nines can become stuck on secondary sources of gratification. In *The Enneagram: A Christian Perspective*, Richard Rohr and Andreas Ebert explain, "Nines seek stimulants and strong sensations from outside because they find it difficult stimulating themselves."[19]

When not in a relationship, Nines dream about finding the perfect partner who will usher them into a wonderful new life. You will often hear a Nine say, "You know things are going to

18. Beesing, et al., *The Enneagram: A Journey of Self Discovery*, 149.
19. Rohr and Ebert, *The Enneagram: A Christian Perspective*, 181.

change when I meet my spouse." They are looking for that special someone who will help them build a life of their own.

The temptation of the Nine is to put themselves down and underestimate themselves. They can appear to be humble, but their motivation is often a desire to escape from revealing too much. They prefer to be present in a room and not seen since their insecurities make them more comfortable staying in the background. They prioritize the need to present themselves as *nothing special*. Those on the outside will notice that Nines sell themselves far too short.

Nines value structure. To everyone's benefit, they can be the hardest working employees when a clear agenda and structure are in place. Familiar routines allow them to accurately predict how much energy will be needed to complete the task and plan accordingly. Deadlines are met with all the energy a Nine can muster. They will put in long hours to meet a deadline and produce quality work.

The Nine's lethargy is found when they must take personal initiative, make plans, and carry them through. This makes them slow down and take it easy, with their sloth-like pace manifesting as procrastination. They are simply overwhelmed by so many decisions. Regarding their own personal life, they often conclude, "There is no reason to wear yourself out." This is the unique brand of inertia found in a Nine.

Because Nines weigh all the pros and cons of a relationship before they commit, it can become difficult for them to give up old relationships. Often, they hold on long after it is time to let go. They are unable to make a move to cut ties. This makes it difficult for new relationships to develop when Nines continue to live in the past of previous alliances. Nines must be encouraged to let go.

> **AS PEOPLE WHO RADIATE PEACE, NINES CAN BRING SERENITY, LOVE, AND HARMONY TO AN OTHERWISE CHAOTIC GATHERING.**

As people who radiate peace, Nines can bring serenity, love, and harmony to an otherwise chaotic gathering. People feel an unexplainable calmness oozing from them.

Nines are helped by someone who will take the initiative to get things going and then invite them to join in. They move toward health when they learn to step forward and assert themselves. This makes them feel liberated, and others enjoy seeing them finally taking a stand. Sometimes Nines just need a little push, a little encouragement, to exercise relational integrity with those with whom they disagree, so they can confront an issue head-on.

UNHEALTHY NINES

While the root sin of the Nine is laziness, other types often fail to understand this accurately. In *The Enneagram in Love and Work*, Helen Palmer explains it this way:

> In the area of social interaction, participating in group activities can be a comforting way to feel included and loved. It can also be the place of greatest laziness of a social Nine, because the energy that could be spent in meeting personal agendas is shunted instead to take part in social activities.[20]

The laziness of this type extends to their personal life only. The Nine's bias is to stay comfortable and keep the peace because they feel that the world won't truly value their efforts anyway. Binge-watching and comfort food can become substitutes for having their own real life with real relationships. For Nines, watching TV gives them an opportunity to check out and put their decisions on pause. Addictions of various kinds are often an ongoing problem

20. Palmer, *The Enneagram in Love and Work*, 226.

for unhealthy Nines. They are snared by temptations because they think that maybe a drink, or some drug, will help to get them going.

Nines desire to totally merge with those they love. They seek a mutual existence where the lines between the individual and the group are blurred or totally disappear. They can absorb another's life into their own like a sponge soaking up water—and yet they are comfortable taking this even one step further. Imagine a sponge that is not only full of water, but totally immersed in it. This is an ideal union for a Nine. Since this depth of interdependence is not desirable to other Enneagram types, Nines wonder, *Why don't you love me as much as I love you?* This feels so unfair to the Nine. They may appear calm, cool, and collected on the outside, but when others don't blend into their life as readily as they do, unhealthy Nines are left with a simmering resentment just beneath the surface.

Nines express their anger in passive-aggressive and stubborn ways. Their anger brews slowly over time. They themselves may not even be conscious of it until days after the incident that set them off, but once it surfaces, Nines will work very hard to avoid open anger. They hate the discomfort of head-on opposition or separation; by being passive-aggressive, they can still have things go their way and remain in control of the conflict.

The silent treatment is one common tactic used by Nines to stubbornly outwait the enemy. They will simply do nothing, and only their silence will let you know you have crossed a line with them. Dragging out a project, being slow to respond to requests, and tuning others out are all responses you can expect from an angry Nine. Should their anger boil over openly, others are shocked by the magnitude of the explosion, and the Nine, in turn, is later embarrassed by it.

HEALTHY NINES

Healthy Nines are attentive to their own needs and desires through some measure of independence. When they expend the personal energy necessary to move forward in their own agendas and goals, they become happy and dynamic. They are giving, adaptive, receptive, and keepers of the peace. These Nines begin supporting the lives of others as their own in great harmony, but not in unison, thus maintaining their own individuality.

> **WHEN NINES EXPEND THE PERSONAL ENERGY NECESSARY TO MOVE FORWARD IN THEIR OWN AGENDAS AND GOALS, THEY BECOME HAPPY AND DYNAMIC.**

Healthy Nines force themselves to look inward to assess their lives. They keep track of where they are in their progress and are highly productive when their lives are structured in this way.

Like all of us, Nines become their best with outside help. The precious Holy Spirit came to lead us into abundant life. Jesus promised, "*When he, the Spirit of truth, comes, he will guide you into all the truth*" (John 16:13). For Nines, a great portion of that truth is to see themselves as they really are. Nines need to take to heart God's promise to provide all of the energy required for living through the power of the Holy Spirit. When tempted to coast through life, Nines need to dig deep and rely on this power. The very same Holy Spirit who came to lead us into truth also came to be our helper. "*The Spirit helps us in our weakness*" (Romans 8:26). Loved ones can help Nines live their best life by challenging them to have their own separate goals, celebrating their progress toward those goals, and reminding them of the importance of paying attention to themselves.

Thankfully, we are not left to fend for ourselves. Jesus promised and delivered the assistance we require. "*But when the Helper comes, whom I will send to you from the Father, the Spirit of truth, who* proceeds from the Father, he will bear witness about me" (John 15:26 ESV). The Holy Spirit reveals Jesus to us, and as we live in His presence, we are changed into His image, into our highest potential.

BIBLICAL EXAMPLE: JONAH

Unhealthy Nines retreat from life, and Jonah is a biblical example of just that. When given an assignment directly from God to go and preach in Nineveh, Jonah set out in the opposite direction. He perfectly demonstrates the downward spiral that Nines take when they withdraw from life and from God's unique purposes for them.

> *But Jonah arose to flee to Tarshish from the presence of the LORD. He went **down** to Joppa, and found a ship going to Tarshish; so he paid the fare, and went **down** into it, to go with them to Tarshish from the presence of the LORD. But the LORD sent out a great wind on the sea, and there was a mighty tempest on the sea, so that the ship was about to be broken up. Then the mariners were afraid; and every man cried out to his god, and threw the cargo that was in the ship into the sea, to lighten the load. But Jonah had gone **down** into the lowest parts of the ship, had lain down, and was fast asleep.*
>
> (Jonah 1:3–5 NKJV)

In the face of death, Jonah remained obstinate—a trait for which Nines are notorious—and chose to be thrown into the sea rather than change his course. (See verse 12.) Even in his rebellion, a gracious God was merciful to him, as He so often is to all of us, and gave Jonah an unlikely life raft: the belly of a great fish! (See verse 17.)

Jonah's stubbornness kept him on a downward spiral. Still obstinate, he progressed further on his descent when he was thrown *down* into the sea and swallowed *down* into the belly of the great fish.

Have you ever wondered how stubborn a Nine can be? It took Jonah three days and three nights in the belly of a great fish, with seaweed wrapped around his head, before he abandoned his stubbornness and cried out to God in repentance! Jonah was on his last stop downward, just before hell itself, before he turned around. Like the prodigal son down in the pigpen, he finally came to his senses. At the very bottom, Jonah moved away from his escapism and turned to God. He prayed:

> "When my life was ebbing away, I remembered you, LORD, and my prayer rose to you, to your holy temple...I, with shouts of grateful praise, will sacrifice to you. What I have vowed I will make good. I will say, 'Salvation comes from the LORD.'" And the LORD commanded the fish, and it vomited Jonah onto dry land. (Jonah 2:7, 9–10)

There is so much to take away from Jonah's story. First, we can learn that God is just waiting on our cry to provide our escape, even at the last stop before hell itself. Second, we cannot outlast God; we are trapped in time, but He is not! It is futile to remain stubborn in our own way of thinking while somehow believing we can win in the end. Fleeing from God's will, being stingy with our energy, and stubbornly wanting our own way will never be a good plan; it is never God's plan.

When healthy Nines integrate toward the Three, the Achiever, and stop selling themselves short, they are capable of great achievements independent of anyone else using their own intuition. They possess a wealth of talent that can stand up on its own merit. They are quite capable of launching their own initiatives and become outright surprised to feel the rush of pleasure and accomplishment when they do. Healthy Nines are an unstoppable force for good who bring cohesiveness to any group.

It is important for Nines to note that it is not enough to merely see an accurate reflection of themselves in the mirror of

13

SO WHO ARE YOU?

We focused most of our time together looking at the Enneagram because I believe it to be the most important personality tool at our disposal. I have laid out all of the descriptions, biblical examples, and testimonies; now it is time for you to find your type. Before you take the Enneagram test, remember that it is imperative for you to be brutally honest with your answers. Your results will not be accurate without candid responses. Please remember that:

1. No one type is better than another.

2. We are all made in the image of God.

3. You are at your very best when you are healthy in the type that God wired you to be.

Please go ahead and take the Enneagram test now. You can find it at: personalitypath.com/free-enneagram-personality-test.

Once you have your results, please go back and review the chapter detailing your Enneagram type. Highlight what really resonates with you and ask the Holy Spirit to speak to you as you go through it with an open mind. As ideas come regarding how you can improve, write those things down. As you understand why you react to others the way you do, be honest with yourself and make a note of that as well. Honest self-reflection is the key to growth.

There are many other resources on the Enneagram that can help you further in knowing how to relate with the other types. Please don't think your new discoveries of the Enneagram need to end here as we move forward to some more personal discoveries. Several other books take you deep into the nuances of each type, but it was necessary for our purposes to simply uncover the top few layers. Share this book with your family and friends and discover their types as well. Doing this will help you to relate to one another with a newfound understanding and empathy.

DISC MODEL

As a second tool on the journey of *Rediscovering You*, you will take the DISC behavioral style test. We will soon begin to put the pieces together to discover the complete picture that is *you*. The Enneagram revealed your personality; now the DISC will unveil behavior.

The DISC model is an acronym for the four main characteristic traits of each behavioral type: D for dominance, I for influence, S for steadiness, and C for conscientiousness. The DISC model can help you understand yourself and others by describing four primary, habitual behaviors. Each person generally has one or two dominant behavioral styles, which is known as their style blend. The strongest behavior is listed first. For example, a person could be SI or IS.

We will take a detailed look into the results of each four styles and then learn how they can be combined with the Enneagram types.

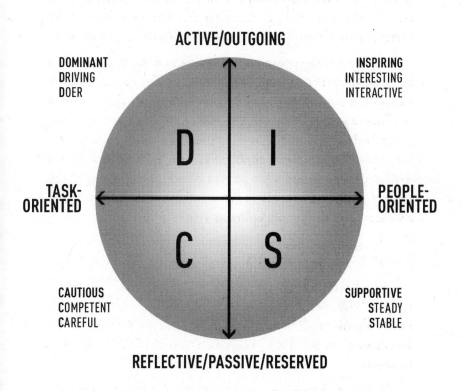

ACTIVE/OUTGOING

DOMINANT
DRIVING
DOER

INSPIRING
INTERESTING
INTERACTIVE

D **I**

TASK-ORIENTED ⟷ **PEOPLE-ORIENTED**

C **S**

CAUTIOUS
COMPETENT
CAREFUL

SUPPORTIVE
STEADY
STABLE

REFLECTIVE/PASSIVE/RESERVED

BEHAVIOR STYLE D (DOMINANT)

PROBABLE ENNEAGRAM TYPE THREE OR EIGHT

Those in the Dominant group, type D, are task-oriented and display active behaviors. They usually focus on results, problem-solving, and the bottom line. Those who score high in the D behavioral style change the world; they are pioneers and attack challenges head-on. It is easy to see how this would be the predominant behavioral style of the Enneagram Three, the Achiever, and Eight, the Challenger.

The D types are direct, demanding, and dominating. If no one makes a decision or steps up to take the lead, the D's in the room will take charge. Enneagram Threes and Eights show no difficulty in making a decision, right or wrong, but it is the Ones, the Reformer, who will make the best decision because they do their due diligence.

> ## THE HIGH D TYPES ARE GREAT AT STARTING PROJECTS AND TAKING INITIATIVE, THOUGH THEY NEED OTHERS AROUND THEM TO HELP WITH COMPLETION.

The high D types are great at starting projects and taking initiative, though they need others around them to help with completion. It is not uncommon for them to have ten things going at once. Enneagram Eights with the D behavioral style want all the details, while Threes only want to see the bottom line. If a high D has no people orientation in their personality blend, they are bulls in a china shop, which is fine with them because they believe, "Things need to be shaken up a bit! It's my way or the highway!"

Task-oriented D's must learn that people are not merely pawns to be used to achieve their goals. The Holy Spirit is needed to help them lift their eyes off the task at times so they can see the people around them. Empathy and understanding are most needed for the driven D's.

Those D's with a high blend of type I (Inspiring) make dynamic leaders. They not only have the drive to meet the challenges at hand, but also have the interpersonal skills needed to inspire and move people toward a common goal. D's with a high type C blend must learn to stop the task train long enough to acknowledge the people along for the ride.

BEHAVIOR STYLE I (INSPIRING)

PROBABLE ENNEAGRAM TYPE FOUR, SEVEN, OR THREE

The behavior style of the I on the DISC assessment test is both outgoing and people-oriented. Inspiring and influential, they usually focus on interacting with people, having fun, or creating excitement. The life of the party, they can influence large numbers of people through their natural ability to motivate others.

High I's need help to stay on task. As long as people are having fun, they will never notice that nothing is getting done. A balanced I uses their influence to inspire others' achievements and advancements. The Enneagram numbers that highly correlate with the I behavioral style are: Fours, the Individualist; Sevens, the Enthusiast; and Threes, the Achiever.

Those with a dominant I behavior style are good at faking it until they make it, but we all know this has its limitations. They mature by learning to be diligent at completing tasks and projects. When surrounded by detail-oriented types, I's can become major powerhouses of progress.

> WHEN SURROUNDED BY DETAIL-ORIENTED TYPES,
> I'S CAN BECOME MAJOR POWERHOUSES OF PROGRESS.

The I's are all about looking good. They are usually quite easy to spot for all of their bright and unique clothing choices. They grow by discovering that life is not about how you look or just about having fun. Healthy I's put their influence to good use when they grow the kingdom of God.

When correcting an I, keep in mind that their greatest fear is looking bad. The wise leader knows the different personality types on their team and is careful to navigate conflict accordingly. It is devastating for a high I to be called out publicly, so finding a way for them to save face while at the same time bringing correction works best.

All relationships improve with our awareness of our own wiring and an awareness of those in our lives. Most in the business and corporate world have long since understood this, but only recently has the church been mindful of this need.

BEHAVIOR STYLE S (SUPPORTIVE)

PROBABLE ENNEAGRAM TYPE TWO, SIX, OR NINE

The S type includes those who are supportive, steady, and people-oriented—the glue of any group. Everyone loves the S in a group because they are not all about themselves, but all about *you*. While the D's and C's are concerned about the task at hand, the S's are concerned about the people. They will be overheard asking, "Is everyone okay? Does everyone have what they need?" They usually focus on preserving relationships and creating or maintaining peace. It is easy to see why Enneagram Twos (the Helper), Sixes (the Loyalist), and Nines (the Peacemaker) are often found in the S category.

Those with the S behavior style are happy to be behind the scenes. They are supportive and work the best one-on-one. They like steady and predictable environments. Though they often appear to be shy at first, S types can keep the conversation going, always sensitive that no one feels left out once they are comfortable with the group.

> **S TYPES ARE SO WELL-LIKED BECAUSE PEOPLE FEEL SAFE AROUND THEM. THEY ARE SENSITIVE TO THE FEELINGS OF OTHERS AND WEIGH THEIR WORDS ACCORDINGLY.**

S types are so well-liked because people feel safe around them. They are sensitive to the feelings of others and weigh their words accordingly. The danger for an S is not standing up for what they believe. They have to know where the line is drawn, that friendship is not everything. This is difficult for the S because their greatest fear is isolation, and their greatest challenge is confrontation.

High S types are so concerned about others' feelings that they have a difficult time making personal decisions. They would rather the group decide. They want to know, "What is everyone else feeling?" Their own needs can become lost in the process.

Those with an SI or IS behavioral style blend must work harder to start and complete tasks. They have wonderful people skills and are all about others, but they can lose themselves in conversation and leave tasks incomplete. What is evident about all of the behavioral types is that they all have their strengths and weaknesses, and we are better together than we are apart.

BEHAVIOR STYLE C (CAUTIOUS)

PROBABLE ENNEAGRAM TYPE ONE OR FIVE

Those who dominate in behavioral style C are task-oriented. They exhibit cautious and careful behaviors with a focus on facts, accuracy, and rules. They are rule keepers and list makers. They find great joy in crossing items off of their to-do list.

Like the high S's, those who are C's often find it hard to make a decision, but for an entirely different reason. The C wonders if they have all the facts and all the details. They wonder what they might have missed. C's want to fill in all of the blanks. Decisions are more difficult for them because their greatest fear is being wrong. The apostle Thomas was a C type. He wanted all the blanks filled in before he would believe that Jesus was resurrected.

> *Now Thomas (also known as Didymus), one of the Twelve, was not with the disciples when Jesus came. So the other disciples told him, "We have seen the Lord!" But he said to them, "Unless I see the nail marks in his hands and put my finger where the nails were, and put my hand into his side, I will not believe." A week later his disciples were in the house again, and Thomas was with them. Though the doors were locked, Jesus came and stood among them and said, "Peace be with you!" Then he said to Thomas, "Put your finger here; see my hands. Reach out your hand and put it into my side. Stop doubting and believe." Thomas said to him, "My Lord and my God!" Then Jesus told him, "Because you have seen me, you have believed; blessed are those who have not seen and yet have believed."* (John 20:24–29)

Jesus understood that Thomas's personality required that all of the blanks be filled in. In *Why Do I Do the Things I Do*, Darrell Parsons noted, "Thomas gets a bad rap for being called the Doubting Apostle. Even today, a skeptical person is called a 'Doubting Thomas.'"[21]

But the Bible doesn't indicate that Jesus was scolding Thomas. Rather, Jesus made the offer to answer all of his questions. Jesus knows our personality type too and meets us right where we are. Parsons goes on to say:

> We see Thomas' competent, compliant, and cautious personality as we read what he said and did as told in the Bible accounts. However, God used Thomas as perhaps the only original Apostle who went outside the Roman Empire to

---

21. Darrell J. Parsons, *Why Do I Do the Things I Do?—Understanding Personalities* (Stafford, VA: Parsons Publishing House, 2011), 75.

preach the Gospel of Jesus Christ. Once convinced of the resurrection, Thomas was unstoppable. He never wavered from his purpose, even to the point of death. He is also believed to have covered the largest area during the time of his ministry, which included modern Persia and India.[22]

Though C's find it hard to make a weighty decision, it is generally the correct answer when they do decide. By doing their due diligence, C's are great at quality control, bookkeeping, and analysis.

> KNOWN FOR THEIR COMPETENCY, A HIGH C WILL OFTEN MISS THE FEELINGS OF THE PEOPLE THEY ARE WORKING WITH BECAUSE THEY CAN ONLY SEE THE TASK.

The C behavioral style is not strong on people skills, but is inclined to get the task done. Known for their competency, a high C will often miss the feelings of the people they are working with because they can only see the task. High C's can frequently be overheard saying, "People shouldn't be so sensitive; we have a job to do, and it has to be done right the first time." They will hurt some feelings along the way, but if you want something done, and done right, delegate it to a C.

The behavioral style of the C type is neat and orderly. They are excellent housekeepers, and everything has its place. They will quickly let you know if you put something out of order. It is quite easy to understand why a C behavioral style is often displayed by an Enneagram One, the Reformer, or a Five, the Investigator.

TAKE THE DISC TEST

It is now time for you to take the test. Once again, remember to be honest with your answers. You can find the DISC test

---

22. Ibid., 77–78.

at: www.onlinepersonalitytests.org/disc or www.123test.com/disc-personality-test/index.php.

FITTING THESE TWO PIECES TOGETHER

Now that you have your behavior type, let's begin to build the puzzle of who you are together. What number are you on the Enneagram? Where are you on the DISC? It is easy to see some obvious parallels between the Enneagram types and the behavioral styles of the four DISC types, but others are more subtle. Having the results of both of these tests will assist you in your journey of self-awareness. They will help you to know your weaknesses and strengths. Our motives become clearer with each new discovery. Don't be afraid to remove the mask to see yourself as you really are.

OUR MOTIVES BECOME CLEARER WITH EACH NEW DISCOVERY. DON'T BE AFRAID TO REMOVE THE MASK TO SEE YOURSELF AS YOU REALLY ARE.

I want to share one personal story with you before we move to the next test. Several years ago, I invited author Darrell Parsons to conduct a personalized DISC testing and training session with me and twelve of my leaders. It was a concentrated effort to make sure we were a well-rounded team. I wanted to make sure we were not just a group with the same strengths and weaknesses.

During one session, Parsons detailed the blind spots of each of our personal behavioral type blends. One by one, he went around the circle and pointed these out based upon our test results. It was very specific to each team member.

As it happened, I was the last of thirteen to get my information. As I listened to Parsons detail the other team members' blind spots, I heard each of them gently push back and say something like, "I don't really think that's me." And all the while, I was screaming inside, "Yes, that *is* you precisely." The precision of Parsons' descriptions of them was uncanny.

Then it was my turn. Parsons began to lay out my blind spots, and almost on cue, I heard my team members' words coming out of my own mouth, "I don't know. I don't think I really do that." That is the moment I had my epiphany. It suddenly dawned on me that I was doing the same thing everyone else did *because* it was, in fact, a *blind spot*. I couldn't see it, just as they could not see theirs. I thought, *What are the odds that he is right about all twelve of them and not correct about me?* Right then and there, I embraced my blind spot and determined to use my mirrors when someone entered it. Knowing my personality type and understanding my behavioral style helps me *fly by the instruments* when I can't see clearly. It helps me shut down my defense mechanisms, to listen first and respond rather than react. Blind spots are always going to be troublesome, but they can be overcome with self-discovery. Also, acknowledging them gives us empathy for the blind spots of others. Relationships are better as a result of such knowledge.

I suggest that you take time to ponder your Enneagram and DISC test results and contemplate what they reveal about you. How do these two pieces fit together? Ask the Holy Spirit to give you insights. Take a deeper look, and don't stop until you know your blind spot. We all have them. What is yours? The more honest you are with yourself, the better all of your relationships will become. We are ready now for our third and final test.

FIVE LOVE LANGUAGES

It's time to talk about love. In 1992, author Gary Chapman wrote a *New York Times* bestseller entitled *The 5 Love Languages: The Secret to Love that Lasts*. In his book, he outlines five general ways people express and experience love, which Chapman calls "love languages." He writes, "My conclusion after many years of marriage counseling is that there are five emotional love languages—five ways that people speak and understand emotional love."[23]

Understanding our personality type, our behavioral style, and our love language equips us for better communication, improved conflict resolution, and harmonious relationships with one another.

> UNDERSTANDING OUR PERSONALITY TYPE, BEHAVIORAL STYLE, AND LOVE LANGUAGE EQUIPS US FOR BETTER COMMUNICATION, IMPROVED CONFLICT RESOLUTION, AND HARMONIOUS RELATIONSHIPS.

Initially, Chapman identified the five love languages to help those in a marriage relationship, but since that time, every relationship has been seen to benefit. For example, parenting is much easier when we understand our child's love language. After thirty years of my own ministry and counseling, I have found Chapman's book to be one of the most valued tools I have used to help others improve their relationships.

The love languages Chapman outlines are: words of affirmation; quality time; receiving gifts; acts of service; and physical touch. He maintains that each person has one primary love language as well as a secondary one. When we speak the right love language, those in a relationship with us feel loved.

Chapman likens our emotional need for love to a "love tank" that must be monitored, like the oil level in an automobile. He points out that a marriage running on an empty love tank can cost you more than trying to run your car without oil.

All love languages are not the same; what works for one person does not necessarily work for another. Some value words of affirmation such as, "I love you" or "That soup you made was delicious,"

---

23. Gary Chapman, *The 5 Love Languages: The Secret to Love that Lasts* (Chicago, IL: Northfield Publishing, 2010), 15.

while others might prefer assistance with chores (an act of service) or a back rub (physical touch).

Discovering and understanding primary and secondary love languages are critical for better relationships. Difficulties occur when we speak the wrong language to one another.

In his book *The 5 Love Languages*, Chapman writes:

Seldom do a husband and wife have the same primary emotional love language. We tend to speak our primary love language, and we become confused when our spouse does not understand what we are communicating. We are expressing our love, but the message does not come through because we are speaking what, to them, is a foreign language.[24]

I discovered this firsthand as a husband with a young family. At that time, my wife and I lived in Daphne, Alabama, near the Gulf Coast. It was August; the heat and humidity were unbearable. One Saturday morning, I decided to show my wife Lezli how much I loved her by cleaning and detailing her van, which we affectionately called "the mommy-mobile."

I worked in the hot sun until the early afternoon, vacuuming the cracker crumbs and cleaning sippy-cup spills from the carpet. I washed and waxed the entire van. Wiping the sweat and the gnats out of my eyes, dropping fifteen pounds, and risking heat stroke, I pressed on until the van looked brand new. Because I am a Three on the Enneagram, I was so proud of my accomplishment. Surely Lezli would know how much I loved her by this tremendous act of service!

Imagine how deflated I became when I finally came into the house, and she said, "Did you decide to finally come into the house? You have been missing all day." When I tried to point out

---

24. Ibid., 16.

the results of my hot, hard, and grueling work, she responded, "I don't care about the van being that clean; we have missed the whole Saturday together." I was so confused, hurt, and disappointed. But in God's providence, someone had just given me a copy of *The 5 Love Languages*. Within just a few pages, I immediately saw my error. I was speaking my own primary love language of "acts of service" to Lezli, whose primary love language is "quality time." I might as well have been speaking Russian to an English speaker! All of that work in the heat was totally unnecessary. I could have filled her love tank by simply spending our day off together. Lesson learned.

> **OUR NATURAL TENDENCY IS TO SPEAK TO OTHERS IN OUR OWN PRIMARY LOVE LANGUAGE. THE PROBLEM IS THAT THEY MAY NOT SPEAK THAT LANGUAGE.**

Our natural tendency is to speak to others in our own primary love language. The problem is that they may not speak that language. Many couples are struggling for this reason alone. We can avoid this pitfall by simply becoming aware that we need to speak in our partner's love language.

Now it's time for you to take the 5 Love Languages test.

Go to: www.5lovelanguages.com/quizzes.

PUTTING IT ALL TOGETHER

Once you have taken the test and discovered your top two love languages, you can begin to reflect on how it fits together with your other results. I suspect that for many, our primary and secondary love languages are closely tied to our Enneagram and DISC types. Here are some examples:

+ Ones' primary or secondary love language may be *quality time* because even with others' imperfections, the Reformer in growth values fun and joy. Ones might also appreciate *words of affirmation* because that love language can silence their inward critic.

+ Many Twos may have *physical touch* as their primary or secondary love language because this says to the Helper, "I know you have your own needs, and I am here for you."

+ Threes, the Achiever, may gravitate to *acts of service* because "my partner loves me enough to help me achieve my goals."

+ Fours could speak the language of *receiving gifts* because this tells the Individualist, "I am special."

+ Fives may also speak this language because a gift indicates you spent a lot of time thinking about the recipient and what they would prefer as a gift, something an Observer would appreciate.

+ Sixes, the Loyalist, may give and receive love through *physical touch*, which says, "I am here for you like a warm security blanket."

+ Sevens' primary love language may be *words of affirmation* because the Enthusiast needs to know they are appreciated for who they are in the present moment.

+ Eights may have *words of affirmation* as their primary or secondary love language due to the Challenger's viewpoint of being in charge.

+ Nines' primary or secondary love language may be *quality time*. For the Peacemaker, this says, "I want to merge my life with yours."

How does your Enneagram type mesh with your primary or secondary love language? Were you able to relate to or recognize these qualities in others?

Please leave me your results at craigwalker.org, and I will respond by sharing the feedback we are receiving.

WHEN CONSCIOUSLY AWARE OF THE WAY WE PROCESS OUR
WORLD AS INDIVIDUALS, WE ARE BETTER EQUIPPED TO
LIVE TOGETHER IN GREATER HARMONY.

At this point, I am confident you have seen the importance of *Rediscovering You*. Relationships flourish with this new information. When consciously aware of the way we process our world as individuals, we are better equipped to live together in greater harmony. Empathy is the by-product of learning the struggles that others face. Greater awareness of their fears and insecurities pulls us outside of our own narrow, self-centered view. Being cognizant of our personal filter removes our blinders and allows us to see beyond our own perspective. We begin to perceive the world as others do by developing our ability to put on the multiple sets of lenses that we call personality types. Like facets of a diamond, we begin to see that there are many ways to look at the same issue. A better understanding of one another is the favorable result.

What is our love language? What motivates us? What is our greatest fear? Understanding the filters through which we view our world enhances our relationships with the people in our lives and our relationship with Christ. Our true motives for why we do what we do have no place to hide when the masks are removed. Lean into each new discovery and watch the favorable results pile up.

14

SELF-DISCOVERY'S APPLICATION

Quite frankly, self-discovery without application is just another rabbit hole we can keep sliding down. It results in nothing more than navel-gazing and narcissism, of which our world has more than enough to go around. By nature, we are egocentric. Left entirely to ourselves, life revolves around us. We only become altruistic by conscious effort. This is where the self-discoveries revealed in this book can do us the most good. We can apply what we learned to improve all of our relationships. We can speak in the love languages that others understand. Though we are all wired very differently, we *can* come together.

Knowing our personality type, behavioral style, or love language does not give us an excuse to say, "I am as the Lord made me." When we try to use any of these as an excuse, we are attempting to absolve ourselves of a responsibility God clearly requires of us. Rather, the wise person will develop their strengths and not leave their personal growth to chance.

All living things grow. Our new awareness should be used as a treasure map that leads us to the higher purposes of God for which He created us. Our wiring is uniquely suited for the purpose that the Lord has for us as individuals and the community He has placed us in.

You bring to the table what no one else can provide. Your DNA is not random—God designed you as a unique person for a specific reason. The psalmist declared, *"I will praise You, for I am fearfully and wonderfully made; marvelous are Your works, and that my soul knows very well"* (Psalm 139:14 NKJV). It is our responsibility to develop and find our place in this world.

God expects us to grow in our Christlikeness by denying our *self* and becoming more like Him. A better understanding of our motivations and the masks we wear removes the shadows where selfishness and self-centeredness can hide. Our personalities are to be developed under the leading of the Holy Spirit and by the power of His Word.

> A BETTER UNDERSTANDING OF OUR MOTIVATIONS AND THE MASKS WE WEAR REMOVES THE SHADOWS WHERE SELFISHNESS AND SELF-CENTEREDNESS CAN HIDE.

All of us must find our rightful place—that place where we can do the most good. We must ask ourselves, "So what is my part in this? Where can I do the best with my particular mix of gifts and talents? How can I be a better spouse, parent, and coworker? How can I help Christ and His church now that I am more aware of my strengths and weaknesses?"

We can revolutionize and rejuvenate how we relate to our spouse, children, friends, coworkers, boss, and pastor by using our new understanding. Many can avoid conflicts and frustration and realize advancements in their careers by developing their communication skills. How many divorces can be avoided by applying some of these tools?

As we have now made every effort to discover the true self by dismantling the false constructs of our identity, we come to this: you are not a mistake, an afterthought, or an accident. There is no *bad* personality type, only healthy and unhealthy versions. Your unique design was given by a loving and caring Creator. You are one of a kind; there is no one else quite like you. When you consider all of the threads of your unique tapestry, this is easy to acknowledge. God gave you your singular design because you need it to fulfill your part of His plan. I pray that you will become all that you can be, a beautiful and redeemed mosaic found in the image of God.

> **GOD GAVE YOU YOUR SINGULAR DESIGN BECAUSE YOU NEED IT TO FULFILL YOUR PART OF HIS PLAN.**

If you wish to go further in discovering God's plan for your life, I encourage you to get a copy of my book *Born for the Extraordinary: When Your Life Aligns with His Purpose*. It will aid you in your journey toward the greatness God has pre-planned for you. All of us were indeed born for the extraordinary!

We have all been tasked with taking the basic building blocks of our personality traits and developing them so that we become all that we can be for Christ and His eternal kingdom. This can only be done when we cooperate with the Holy Spirit and focus on *"Christ in you, the hope of glory"* (Colossians 1:27). He is the only One who can complete us. It is my earnest prayer that you will take what you have learned and fulfill your God-given destiny in its entirety. I pray that you will love more deeply, forgive more readily, and become all you were hardwired to become in Christ.

15

A WARNING FOR PEOPLE OF FAITH

Religion is a perfect hiding place for a false self-image. In some cases, attending religious services and activities only serves to polish the mask and hide the truth of a wicked heart. While attending church is essential to the growth and maturity of a follower of Christ, if *showing up* is merely a part of a false construct of who we are, it becomes more dangerous than not attending in the first place.

This is why Jesus was so tough on those who had only a *form* of religion. Jesus said to them, *"Woe to you, teachers of the law and Pharisees, you hypocrites! You are like whitewashed tombs, which look beautiful on the outside but on the inside are full of the bones of the dead and everything unclean"* (Matthew 23:27). A change that occurs from the outside-in is in direct opposition to the work of Christ. This kind of change leads to the same self-deception and hypocrisy that Jesus despised in those scribes and Pharisees.

A CHANGE THAT OCCURS FROM THE OUTSIDE-IN IS IN DIRECT OPPOSITION TO THE WORK OF CHRIST.

Finding clarity in our true selves through the maze of religion is not a simple task. As the authors note in *The Enneagram: A Christian Perspective*:

> There's nothing on which people are so fixated on as on their self-image. We are literally prepared to go through hell just so we don't have to give it up. It determines most of what we do or don't do, say or don't say, what we occupy ourselves with and what we don't. We are all affected by it.[25]

True motives are often more difficult to discern for people of faith than they are for those who are not religious.

The real irony is that in the church—the place where people can hear the Word of God, our most powerful tool for removing the mask—you will find many steeped in self-deception. In fact, churches and religious institutions are often popular hangouts for what author M. Scott Peck called "the people of the lie."[26] The deluded are found here because they must continually prop up the false façades they have built to convince themselves and the people around them that they are good. Rather than trying to *be* good, they merely want to *appear* to be good. As their everyday lives contradict their false identities, they find new ways to counter the mounting evidence of their masks. They seek to conceal hard self-truths through church attendance and activities.

But God knows they are not sincere.

For the word of God is alive and active. Sharper than any double-edged sword, it penetrates even to dividing soul and spirit,

---

25. Rohr and Ebert, *The Enneagram: A Christian Perspective*, 26.
26. M. Scott Peck, *People of the Lie: The Hope for Healing Human Evil* (New York: Touchstone, 1983).

*joints and marrow; it judges the thoughts and attitudes of
the heart. Nothing in all creation is hidden from God's sight.
Everything is uncovered and laid bare before the eyes of him to
whom we must give account.*   (Hebrews 4:12–13)

So how is it that people can hide where the Bible is being
preached? The apostle James wrote that God's Word can only
keep us from self-deception when put into practice. Faith without works is dead and self-deceiving. Scripture gives us an accurate
reflection of who we really are, only if we know it *and* walk it out:

*But be doers of the word, and not hearers only, deceiving your-
selves. For if anyone is a hearer of the word and not a doer,
he is like a man observing his natural face in a mirror; for
he observes himself, goes away, and immediately forgets what
kind of man he was. But he who looks into the perfect law of
liberty and continues in it, and is not a forgetful hearer but a
doer of the work, this one will be blessed in what he does.*

(James 1:22–25 NKJV)

Self-deception is not exposed without action. The real danger
is in hearing instruction from God's Word and then not acting
upon it. This leads deeper into the dreaded rabbit hole—and it
is truly frightening how deep it can go. It was self-deceived religious people who put Jesus to death while believing they were
doing God's work. Those found in this category possess the most
extreme cases of mistaken identity. They are righteous in their
own eyes, but evil in their hearts. Jesus said of them, *"On the outside you appear to people as righteous but on the inside you are full of
hypocrisy and wickedness"* (Matthew 23:28). In this state, people
are truly lost because they don't see their real condition.

IT WAS SELF-DECEIVED RELIGIOUS PEOPLE WHO PUT JESUS TO DEATH
WHILE BELIEVING THEY WERE DOING GOD'S WORK.

It is clear that Jesus spent a great deal of time addressing those who didn't act upon what they heard. He boldly called them hypocrites and warned His disciples not to follow their example, saying, "*Be on your guard against the yeast of the Pharisees, which is hypocrisy*" (Luke 12:1). Jesus warned that the scribes and Pharisees "*tie up heavy, cumbersome loads and put them on other people's shoulders, but they themselves are not willing to lift a finger to move them*" (Matthew 23:4). These hypocrites were all talk and no action.

> *Then Jesus told this story to some who had great confidence in their own righteousness and scorned everyone else: "Two men went to the Temple to pray. One was a Pharisee, and the other was a despised tax collector. The Pharisee stood by himself and prayed this prayer: 'I thank you, God, that I am not like other people—cheaters, sinners, adulterers. I'm certainly not like that tax collector! I fast twice a week, and I give you a tenth of my income.' But the tax collector stood at a distance and dared not even lift his eyes to heaven as he prayed. Instead, he beat his chest in sorrow, saying, 'O God, be merciful to me, for I am a sinner.' I tell you, this sinner, not the Pharisee, returned home justified before God. For those who exalt themselves will be humbled, and those who humble themselves will be exalted."* (Luke 18:9–14 NLT)

The Pharisee in this story could not discern the ugliness of his own sin. Pride blinded his eyes to his own spiritual condition. Since evil people may hide in churches and hypocrites are spiritually blind, rather than pointing the finger, it behooves every churchgoer to ask themselves, "Am I one of them? Am I blind to my own condition? Have I fallen down the rabbit hole?"

The people of the lie have not gone away. "*By their fruit you will recognize them*" (Matthew 7:16). They are the ones who go to church on Sunday, even singing in the choir, and then yell obscenities at a harried store clerk on Monday.

In all his goodness, Jesus demonstrated the remedy for breaking self-deception. He dealt with it directly and removed all the places where it could hide. Jesus forced people to see their duplicity.

> *Later they sent some of the Pharisees and Herodians to Jesus to catch him in his words. They came to him and said, "Teacher, we know that you are a man of integrity. You aren't swayed by others, because you pay no attention to who they are; but you teach the way of God in accordance with the truth. Is it right to pay the imperial tax to Caesar or not? Should we pay or shouldn't we?" But Jesus knew their hypocrisy. "Why are you trying to trap me?" he asked. "Bring me a denarius and let me look at it."*   (Mark 12:13–15)

Jesus refused to allow them to hide behind the mask of religion. He knows that if we cannot see ourselves as we truly are, we cannot be the people He wants us to be. In *People of the Lie*, M. Scott Peck wrote:

> The essential component of evil is not the absence of a sense of sin or imperfection but the unwillingness to tolerate that sense. At one and the same time, the evil are aware of their evil and desperately trying to avoid the awareness. Rather than blissfully lacking a sense of morality, like the psychopath, they are continually engaged in sweeping the evidence of their evil under the rug of their own consciousness…The problem is not a defect of conscience but the effort to deny the conscience its due. We become evil by attempting to hide from ourselves. The wickedness of the evil is not committed directly, but indirectly as a part of this cover-up process. Evil originates not in the absence of guilt but in the effort to escape it. It often happens, then, that the evil may be recognized by its very disguise. The lie can be perceived before the misdeed it is designed to hide—the cover-up before the fact. We see the smile that

hides the hatred, the smooth and oily manner that masks the fury, the velvet glove that covers the fist.[27]

We become evil by attempting to hide from ourselves and our convictions. The lie is designed not so much to mislead others as it is to deceive ourselves. This is why all of us should practice better self-awareness, for we are so easily self-deceived.

We need help outside of ourselves. Jesus came to redeem us and change us from the inside out. Then He sent the Holy Spirit to guide us into all truth. The Holy Spirit came to convict us of sin and reveal even our deepest hidden motives. Through repentance, we no longer need to retreat from our Creator in guilt and shame. We no longer need to hide behind the masks we wear, covering up our nakedness. We can come clean before our loving heavenly Father, knowing that our true identity is found simply in being His child.

It is my great hope that the Holy Spirit will use this book and the tools described within it to liberate many from the false-self and into the freedom of becoming true image-bearers of God. You are beautiful in Christ as you abide in Him.

---

27. Peck, *People of the Lie*, 76.

ABOUT THE AUTHOR

Craig Walker is an author, pastor, church consultant, coach for pastors, and leader of the multi-campus Upward Church in Pensacola, Florida; Norfolk and Williamsburg, Virginia; and Kampala, Uganda. Through Wifi Jesus, he preaches in 111 nations weekly and is a regular contributor for GodTV.

He and his wife Lezli are former missionaries to China and Czechoslovakia.

Craig received his master's degree in theology from International Seminary in Florida. He is the author of several books, including *Born for the Extraordinary: When Your Life Aligns with His Purpose*, *Catch: The Art of Fishing for Souls*, *Taboo: God and Money*, and *Last Minute God*, which has been printed in thirteen languages.

Craig and Lezli are the parents of two grown children, Christian and Candace, and reside in Pensacola, Florida.

To connect with Craig, visit craigwalker.org.

Welcome to Our House!

We Have a Special Gift for You

It is our privilege and pleasure to share in your love of Christian books. We are committed to bringing you authors and books that feed, challenge, and enrich your faith.

To show our appreciation, we invite you to sign up to receive a specially selected **Reader Appreciation Gift**, with our compliments. Just go to the Web address at the bottom of this page.

God bless you as you seek a deeper walk with Him!

WE HAVE A GIFT FOR YOU. VISIT:

whpub.me/nonfictionthx

WHITAKER
HOUSE